P9-DZX-869

THE
DESPERATE
HOUSEWIVES
Cookbook

THE DESPERATE HOUSEWIVES Cookbook

Juicy Dishes and Saucy Bits

RECIPES BY Christopher Styler

TEXT BY Scott S. Tobis

BASED ON THE SERIES CREATED BY Marc Cherry

HYPERION

NEW YORK

Library of Congress Cataloging-in-Publication Data

The Desperate housewives cookbook: juicy dishes and saucy bits.

    p. cm.

  ISBN 1-4013-0277-7

  1. Cookery. 2. Desperate housewives.

  TX714.D493 2006

  641.5–dc22

2006043376

Hyperion books are available for special promotions and premiums.

For details contact Michael Rentas, Assistant Director, Inventory Operations,

Hyperion, 77 West 66th Street, 12th floor, New York, New York 10023, or call 212-456-0133.

FIRST EDITION

BOOK DESIGN BY DEBORAH KERNER / DANCING BEARS DESIGN

10   9   8   7   6   5   4   3   2   1

I'D LIKE TO DEDICATE THIS BOOK
TO ALL THE TASTY MORSELS
WHO HAVE MADE MY LIFE SO DELICIOUS . . .

BRENDA, MARCIA, TERI, EVA,
NICOLLETTE, AND FELICITY.

—MARC CHERRY

CONTENTS

Susan 72

Gabrielle 130

Lynette 172

For ordinary people, food is heaven.
—CHINESE PROVERB

INTRODUCTION

IT IS SAID THAT VARIETY IS THE SPICE OF LIFE. OR IS IT MORE ACCURATE to suggest that spices are the very things that make our lives more interesting and varied?

The kitchens on Wisteria Lane are no exception. And it is there, right along with the spice racks, that the rich and varied personalities of our favorite housewives can be found. The secrets, murderous plans, and love affairs that were discussed in the kitchens of ancient queens, saints, and politicians pale in comparison to those of the women of Wisteria Lane, who each have plenty of juicy tales of intrigue, lust, and hunger to tell. Susan Mayer, Bree Van De Kamp, Lynette Scavo, Gabrielle Solis . . . and, lest we forget, the town slut (but not technically a housewife), Edie Britt—in each of their kitchens, we can glimpse their true selves. For who these women are dictates what foods they make. Isn't that true for all of us?

Take Bree Van De Kamp, the housewife whose kitchen is the most immaculate, well-stocked, and busiest on Wisteria Lane. In Bree's kitchen, the forty-two-inch stainless steel side-by-side Thermador refrigerator and the thirty-six-inch gas stovetop with built-in griddle resting on the oversize island are not just for show. These items, like everything else in her ultramodern yet classic kitchen, are part of what makes Bree tick. They define her as a woman who lives and breathes food, in terms of both taste and presentation. When Bree's life is good, she uses food to celebrate; when things are difficult, she uses cooking to escape.

While the other women of Wisteria Lane certainly enjoy their favorite dishes, no one dares compete with Bree—or her kitchen.

Divorced, single mother Susan Mayer has "limited" cooking skills, though she is always eager to try. Lynette Scavo is too much of a pragmatist and far too busy with her demanding job and her family even to entertain the notion of being a gourmand. Former model Gabrielle Solis certainly enjoys haute cuisine, but simply can't be bothered with the arduous process of preparing it herself. Only Edie Britt, who has created some tempting dishes as part of her seduction of various men, can come close to competing in the same arena as Bree where the kitchen is concerned.

Wisteria Lane is a picture-perfect street, where soufflés never fall and the grass on the lawns is never more than two inches high—and always a vibrant green. It's a place where the newspapers are delivered to the front door before anyone arises, a community where all of the neighbors get along . . . at least, this is what everyone pretends is going on. We all know the truth: Nothing is perfect.

Inevitably, secrets do reveal themselves. The lawns may be verdant—but the grass might actually be painted green. The ideal house might create the illusion of perfection, but the foundation is falling apart because of a termite infestation. Inside the kitchens of our favorite housewives, the soufflé does, in fact, fall far too often (except in the Van De Kamp household). With cooking—as with life—it's only with practice and a sense of humor when things fail that we can learn to get it right.

From Susan's classically awful Macaroni and Cheese (somehow burned and undercooked at the same time) to Gabrielle's Quesadillas (tasting uncannily like the ones served at her favorite Mexican restaurant in the city) to Lynette's Buttermilk-Soaked Fried Chicken, the food on Wisteria Lane has a flavor quite unique to this unusual community.

The recipes on the following pages run the gamut of the cooking styles, cultures, and abilities of the women of Wisteria Lane. So as you read *The Desperate Housewives Cookbook*, you will be reminded that we are all different. If you are like Bree, perhaps your meal will be a perfect balance of taste and presentation. And if you are similar to Susan, perhaps it's best to have a wealth of spices handy to cover up the imperfections. And that's okay! Because it is in our differences that we find the very spice that makes life worth living.

THE DESPERATE HOUSEWIVES Cookbook

Bree

Presentation is everything

in Bree Van De Kamp's home. From the unique doorbell
chimes that alert her of a visitor's arrival to the elegant
styling that informs each individual room in her house,
everything looks perfect. And dinner at Bree's house is
certainly no exception.

Anything worth doing is worth doing right. Or so
Bree Van De Kamp has repeated to her family a thousand
times. One's house is not truly clean unless it's spotless; the
party is not worth having unless everyone has a great time;
and the food is not worth preparing unless it requires great
skill and showcases Bree's culinary talent.

So, in Bree's world, meals are not about convenience.
They are about simmering, braising, puréeing, steeping,
chopping, and flambéing.

Queen of the kitchen since she was a little girl, Bree
Van De Kamp defines herself by the masterpieces she
creates in the kitchen. First she was a doting doctor's wife
who helped her husband move up the ranks at the hospital
by hosting the most perfect dinner parties. Then she
became a loving mother who always had a hot breakfast
prepared from scratch and a lunch bag full of the tastiest
foods ready for her kids every morning—all made to her
exacting specifications. She became president of the PTA
and the Junior League because no one could outdo Bree
Van De Kamp. But over time all those things left her,
and the only one left intact was that she was always a
great cook.

Bree is the first to whip up a crème brûlée with ease,
and she never thinks twice about peaks for her egg whites.
But she would never make something as gauche as a tuna

fish sandwich or open a can of SpaghettiOs and serve it as a meal. In a world of fast food, TV dinners, and microwaves, Bree stands alone as a tribute to a bygone era. She scorns people who buy ready-made salad, precut fruit, or any form of frozen dinners. She still believes that food is an experience, in both preparation and consumption, and anything less than full participation reduces our enjoyment of food and life. A family is not whole unless they dine together on a meal that took all day to prepare.

Bree also insists that food will solve almost every problem that comes her way. If her daughter, Danielle, is acting up, Bree whips up a chocolate banana malt. If Andrew seems more sullen than usual, she makes his favorite dish. Her late husband and her children always took her skill and thoughtfulness for granted, which is ironic since she worked so hard in an effort to please and impress them.

Recently, many of Bree's preconceived notions about the world have been changing. Sometimes she believes that the only thing that she can still hold on to is a perfectly executed recipe. The rest of us mere mortals just stop and stare at anyone who can do what Bree does . . . Or we merely hope to be invited over to their house for dinner.

Basil Purée Soup

2 medium leeks

2 tablespoons unsalted butter

1 medium yellow onion, cut into ½-inch dice

3 cups Chicken Broth (page 37) or store-bought chicken broth

1 large bunch basil, leaves removed from stems
   (about 4 cups lightly packed leaves)

½ to 1 cup heavy cream

Salt and freshly gound black pepper

2 to 3 lemon wedges

1. Cut the dark green leaves off the leeks and discard them. Cut off the roots and slice the leeks in half lengthwise. Wash the leek halves under cool running water, being sure to remove all the sand and grit from between the layers. Cut the leeks crosswise into ½-inch pieces and drain thoroughly.

2. Melt the butter in a heavy 2 ½- to 3-quart saucepan over medium-low heat. Stir in the leeks and onion. Cook, stirring occasionally, until the leeks are tender and the onion is softened but not browned, about 8 minutes. Pour in the broth, increase the heat to high, and bring to a boil. Adjust the heat so the liquid is simmering and cook, covered, 5 minutes.

3. Strain the soup into a bowl. Put the leeks and onion in a blender jar and blend at low speed until smooth. With the motor running, pour in enough of the strained liquid to make a very smooth purée. If serving the soup right away, add the basil to the blender and blend until completely smooth. Scrape the mixture from the blender into the saucepan and add the rest of the liquid from the bowl. Heat just to simmering and stir in ½ cup cream. Taste and add all or part of the remaining cream, if desired. Season with salt and pepper and squeeze in lemon juice from the wedges to taste. If you'd like to prepare the soup partially in

CONTINUED

advance, scrape the leek and onion purée (before adding the basil) into the liquid remaining in the bowl. Refrigerate this soup base up to 2 days. To serve, purée about half the chilled base with the basil, then pour into the remaining base. Heat, season, and serve as above.

Chilled Basil Purée Soup

Make the soup base and chill as described above. When thoroughly chilled, blend the base and basil until smooth, then stir in the cream and season with salt, pepper, and lemon juice to taste.

MAKES 4 CUPS • SERVES 4 AS A FIRST COURSE

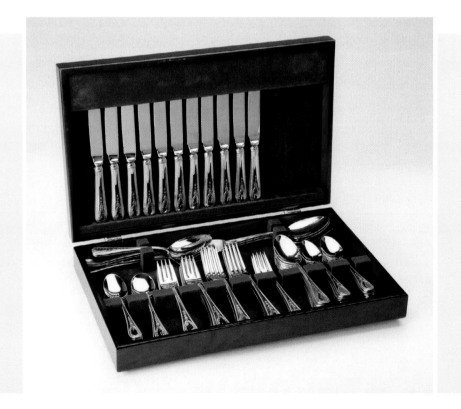

Bree Van De Kamp

freshly squeezed orange juice

organic unbleached flour

brown eggs

Wheat bread

Chicken breast

fresh broccoli

pruning shears for the garden (very sharp)

Loin of pork

Ty Nant bottled water

shallots

Monkfish

fresh salmon

insecticide (extra strength)

Leeks

brown rice

Shiitake mushrooms

garlic

green beans

Roquefort cheese

Sauerkraut

unsalted butter

Rack of lamb

fresh fennel

Crème fraîche

10-gauge shotgun shells

shotgun sling

Tomato Bisque

This is an elegant soup, satiny smooth and rich in flavor. It can be served as is or with a drizzle of cream, a sprig of dill, or a flotilla of croutons. Because it is so chic and pretty and because it can be made completely in advance, it is a perfect candidate for a dinner party first course.

3 tablespoons unsalted butter

2 small celery stalks, trimmed and finely chopped (about ⅔ cup)

2 medium leeks, cleaned (see page 5) and finely chopped
   (about 3 ½ cups)

Two 28-ounce cans round (not plum) tomatoes, with their liquid

¼ cup dry sherry, plus more for drizzling into the finished soup

⅓ to ½ cup light cream

Salt and freshly ground black pepper

1. Heat the butter in a heavy large saucepan over medium heat just until it begins to brown in spots. Add the celery and leeks and cook, stirring, until wilted, about 5 minutes. Meanwhile, pour the tomatoes into a bowl. Pull out the core from each tomato and discard. Crush the tomatoes roughly with your hands.

2. Add the sherry to the pan, bring to a boil, and cook until almost completely evaporated. Add the tomatoes and liquid and bring to a boil. Adjust the heat so the liquid is simmering. Cover and cook 20 minutes. Let sit off the heat until cooled to room temperature.

3. Purée the soup in a food processor until very smooth. Pass the soup through a fine-mesh sieve into a saucepan large enough to hold it comfortably. Use the back of a ladle to push as much of the purée as possible through the sieve and discard the solids left in the sieve. Stir in the cream to taste. The soup can be prepared to this point up to 2 days in advance.

4. Reheat the soup over low heat. Add a few spritzes of sherry and season to taste with salt and pepper. Serve hot.

MAKES 4 CUPS • SERVES 4 AS A FIRST COURSE

Corn Chowder

6 ears corn or 3 cups frozen corn kernels

3 tablespoons unsalted butter

2 small yellow onions, finely diced (about 1 ½ cups)

1 small red bell pepper, cored, seeded, and finely diced
  (about 1 ½ cups)

1 celery stalk, trimmed and finely diced (about ½ cup)

Salt

3 cups Chicken Broth (page 37) or store-bought chicken broth

1 large baking potato, peeled and cut into ½-inch dice (about 2 cups)

½ teaspoon dried thyme

1 bay leaf

1 cup light cream

3 scallions, trimmed and very thinly sliced

Freshly ground black pepper

1. If using fresh corn, shuck the corn and rub off as much of the silk as possible. Cut the stalk flat with the bottom of the ear and stand the ear up on a cutting board. Run a knife blade from the top to the bottom of the ear, removing as many of the kernels as you can without cutting into the cob. Set the kernels aside.

2. Melt the butter in a heavy 4- to 5-quart pot over medium heat until foaming. Stir in the onions, bell pepper, and celery and season lightly with salt. Cook, stirring, until wilted, about 6 minutes. Add the chicken broth, potato, thyme, and bay leaf. Bring to a boil, then adjust the heat so the liquid is simmering. Cover and cook until the potatoes are almost tender, about 6 minutes.

3. Stir in the cream and corn. Season to taste with salt. Bring to a simmer and cook until all the vegetables are tender, about 5 minutes. Stir in the scallions, season with salt and pepper, and serve hot.

SERVES 6

Note: If you'd like a vegetarian soup, substitute homemade or store-bought vegetable stock for the chicken broth or make this simple broth: After removing the kernels from the cobs, put the cobs in a pot large enough to hold them snugly. Cover with cold water and bring to a boil. Adjust the heat to simmering and cook 30 minutes. Drain the liquid and use 3 cups of it in place of the chicken broth.

Salad of Boston Lettuce with Chili-Toasted Walnuts, Blue Cheese, and Oranges

Salads are most fun when each mouthful contains a variety of flavors, textures, and colors. Here is one example, with its sweet-spicy-crunchy mix. The chili-toasted walnuts, made with walnut halves instead of pieces, would make a nice nibble on their own.

FOR THE WALNUTS

⅔ cup walnut pieces

1 teaspoon vegetable oil

½ teaspoon sugar

¼ teaspoon chili powder

¼ teaspoon salt

FOR THE SALAD

2 heads Boston lettuce

2 Valencia oranges

2 teaspoons Dijon mustard

5 to 6 tablespoons olive oil

Salt and freshly ground black pepper

2 ounces finely crumbled blue cheese (about ½ cup)

1. Preheat the oven to 350°F. Toss the walnuts and oil together in a small bowl until the walnuts are evenly coated. Sprinkle the sugar, chili powder, and salt over the nuts and toss again. Spread the walnuts out on a baking sheet and bake until aromatic and lightly toasted, about 12 minutes. Remove and cool.

2. Remove any wilted or yellow leaves from the lettuces. Twist and pull out the cores. Separate the heads into leaves and trim as much of the white core from each leaf as you like. Tear larger leaves into bite-size pieces and leave smaller center leaves whole. Wash the leaves in plenty of cold water, drain thoroughly, and dry, preferably in a salad spinner. The lettuce can be prepared up to several hours before serving. Store in a plastic bag in the vegetable drawer of the refrigerator.

CONTINUED

3. Peel the oranges and cut the segments from them, working over a bowl to catch the juice. (See step 1 of the Ambrosia recipe, page 234.) Remove the orange segments with a slotted spoon. Whisk the mustard into the juice. Pour the oil into the bowl in a slow stream, whisking constantly. Season to taste with salt and pepper.

4. To serve: Toss the lettuce, blue cheese, and orange segments together gently in a serving bowl. Drizzle the dressing over the salad and toss again. Scatter the walnuts over the top and serve.

SERVES 4

Practical Kitchen Terms

Turn off the Food Channel. Put down those Martha Stewart cookbooks cluttering your kitchen. Forget asking for the recipe for that fancy entrée that your neighbor said was "so easy" to replicate in your kitchen. They're all lying to you. Cooking is tough. It's time-consuming, it's demanding, it's needlessly complex.

The truth is, preparing cuisine for your family doesn't have to be that complex. Much of the confusion comes from the terminology itself. Whether the words are in another language (mostly French and Italian), needlessly fancy, or overly complicated, these terms often have very simple definitions. And it's my goal to remove some of the mystique in the kitchen.

What follows is a list of culinary terms that would send a shiver down the spine of a novice chef. But there is no need for anyone to be scared away. Once you've learned the simple truths about these terms, the kitchen should be a far less frightening place for you.

Al Dente

Simply put, it means firm pasta. The word is nothing more than the Italian term for "to the tooth," which refers to the firm but tender consistency a perfectly cooked piece of pasta will have.

Blanch

To place foods in boiling water briefly either to partially cook them (e.g., string beans, peas) or to aid in the removal of the skin (e.g., nuts, peaches, tomatoes).

Braise

A cooking method where food (usually meat) is first browned in oil, then slowly cooked in a liquid (wine, stock, or water).

Bruschetta

Basically a fancy version of toast. It is most commonly topped with tomatoes and basil for good measure. Of course, if you follow the traditional model, it involves the elaborate ritual of rubbing slices of bread with garlic cloves, then drizzling the bread with extra-virgin olive oil, adding salt and pepper to it, then finally heating it in the oven until toasted.

Demiglace

A thick, intensely flavored, glossy brown sauce that is served with meat or poultry or used as a base for other sauces. It is made by thickening a rich veal stock, enriching it with diced vegetables, tomato paste, and Madeira or sherry, then reducing it until concentrated.

Drawn butter

A needlessly confusing term for what is essentially an overly fancy form of melted butter.

Gnocchi

An Italian dumpling made with potato and flour, plain and simple. Don't let the word scare you, since it's delicious and well worth the minor hassle.

Macerate

To soak a fruit in liquor or wine. This softens the fruit while releasing its juices and absorbing the macerating liquid's flavor.

Pancetta

Simply put, an unsmoked version of bacon. A little more crudely put, it's an Italian cured meat made from the belly of the pig, the same cut used for bacon. It is salted and lightly spiced, but not smoked.

Polenta

A mush made from coarse yellow cornmeal that is a staple of northern Italy. As versatile as pasta, polenta can be served hot with various toppings. It can be molded, then cut into squares and fried or grilled.

Prosciutto

One of the most treasured cured hams in the world, which has been produced since the early days of the Roman Empire. Prosciutto is cured—not smoked or cooked—ham, and that accounts for its unique flavor, color, and texture.

In the end, remember to enjoy your time in the kitchen. It shouldn't be difficult. In fact, the process can be relatively painless. And if you're lucky, it can even be *fun*.

Bon Appétit !

Finger Sandwiches

These are the perfect companion to afternoon tea. Bree enjoys serving them to fellow members of the club. She prepares them an hour or two in advance, keeping them wrapped tightly in plastic and refrigerated.

Olive–Cream Cheese

¼ cup small pimiento-stuffed olives
⅓ cup cream cheese, at room temperature
Hot red pepper sauce
8 slices bread (see Note on page 18)

Finely chop the olives by hand or in a food processor using quick on/off pulses. Beat together with the cream cheese and hot pepper sauce to taste until evenly blended. Spread one quarter of the olive mixture over each of 4 bread slices. Top with 4 more slices. Trim the crusts from the sandwiches and cut each into 4 squares or triangles.

MAKES 16 FINGER SANDWICHES

Cucumber–Dill Butter

36 dime-thin slices hothouse or small Kirby cucumbers, or as needed
Salt
3 tablespoons unsalted butter, at room temperature
1 tablespoon finely chopped fresh dill
8 slices bread (see Note on page 18)

1. Spread the cucumber slices out in a single layer on a sheet of paper towel. Sprinkle lightly with salt and let stand.

2. Beat the butter and dill together in a small bowl. Spread the butter onto one side of 8 slices of bread. There will be enough butter to coat each slice very lightly.

CONTINUED

3. Arrange the cucumber slices overlapping very slightly over 4 of the bread slices. Top with the remaining bread, pressing each gently. Cut off the crusts and cut each sandwich into 4 squares or triangles.

MAKES 16 FINGER SANDWICHES

Smoked Salmon–Caper

3 tablespoons mayonnaise
1 tablespoon drained tiny (nonpareil) capers, finely chopped
Few grinds of freshly ground black pepper
8 slices bread (see Note below)
4 ounces thinly sliced smoked salmon

1. Stir the mayonnaise and capers together in a small bowl. Season to taste with pepper. Spread the mayo onto one side of 8 slices of bread. There will be enough mayo to coat each slice lightly.

2. Arrange the smoked salmon slices to cover 4 of the bread slices in a more or less even layer. Top with the remaining bread, pressing each gently. Cut off the crusts and cut each sandwich into 4 squares or triangles.

MAKES 16 FINGER SANDWICHES

Note: Choose a good-quality, thinly sliced packaged bread. Pepperidge Farm makes both wheat and white "very thin" loaves that are perfect for these.

Dressed-Up Deviled Eggs

FOR THE EGGS

  12 extra-large eggs

  ½ cup plus 2 tablespoons mayonnaise

  1 teaspoon dry mustard

  1 teaspoon Worcestershire sauce

  ½ teaspoon salt

  Hot red pepper sauce to taste (optional)

FOR DRESSING UP

  Bright green dill fronds

  Drained small (nonpareil) capers

  Paprika

  Anchovies, cut lengthwise into thin strips

  Black or green olives, pitted if necessary and cut into thin strips

  Bottled pimientos, cut into thin strips about 1 inch long

1. Put the eggs into a saucepan large enough to hold them comfortably. Pour in enough cold water to cover the eggs by 3 inches and bring to a boil over high heat. Adjust the heat so the water is simmering and cook 11 minutes.

2. Carefully pour off the hot water from the pan and put the pan under cold running water. Let cold water run over the eggs 3 minutes. Roll the eggs one at a time gently against a hard surface to lightly crack the shell. Return to the water and let stand until completely cool.

3. Peel the eggs carefully to avoid removing any of the egg white along with the shells. Cut the eggs in half lengthwise through the yolk, nudging the yolks into a small mixing bowl as you go. Be careful to keep the whites intact. Line the whites, cut-side up, on a paper towel–lined baking sheet or tray.

CRACKING THE SHELL AND RETURNING THEM TO WATER MAKES HARD-BOILED EGGS EASIER TO PEEL.

4. Make the filling: Add the mayonnaise, mustard, Worcestershire sauce, salt, and hot red pepper sauce, if using, to the yolks. Beat with a handheld mixer until light and fluffy. The whites and filling can be prepared up to a day in advance.

CONTINUED

Cover the whites with damp paper towels, then with plastic wrap. Scrape the filling into a container and refrigerate filling and whites until needed.

5. To serve: Scrape the filling into a pastry bag fitted with a star tip. Set the whites on a platter before filling. (It's easier and less messy than trying to move filled eggs. A scattering of finely shredded lettuce such as romaine will also keep the eggs in place on the platter.) Pipe the filling into the hollows of the whites. (Alternatively, spoon the filling into the whites.) Decorate the filling with a variety of the toppings. Curl the anchovies or pimientos, add a sprinkle of paprika to olive- or caper-topped eggs—have fun! Let stand at room temperature 15 minutes before serving.

MAKES 24

Caesar Salad

3 hard-boiled eggs (see step 1 of Dressed-Up Deviled Eggs, page 19)

¼ cup lemon juice

1 teaspoon Worcestershire sauce

3 flat anchovy fillets

1 garlic clove, peeled and smashed

3 tablespoons grated Parmesan cheese

2 teaspoons mustard

¾ cup extra-virgin olive oil

FOR THE SALAD

3 hearts of Romaine

Parmesan cheese, grated or shaved into shards with a vegetable peeler

Croutons (see box opposite)

Flat anchovy fillets (optional)

1. Make the dressing: Combine the hard-boiled egg yolks (the whites can be chopped and added to this or another salad), lemon juice, Worcestershire sauce, 3 anchovies, garlic, 3 tablespoons Parmesan cheese, and mustard in a small food processor. Process until smooth. With the motor running, pour the oil into the yolk mixture in a slow, steady stream until it is incorporated and the dressing is smooth. The dressing can be made up to a day in advance. Store covered in the refrigerator.

2. Trim the dark green tips and the core and bottom inch or so from the Romaine. Cut the heads in quarters lengthwise, then crosswise into 1 ½-inch pieces. Wash the lettuce thoroughly and dry it well, preferably in a salad spinner. Store the salad loosely packed in a plastic bag in the vegetable drawer until needed.

3. To serve: Empty the lettuce into a large mixing or serving bowl. Fluff it up, then scatter the grated or shaved Parmesan cheese over the lettuce and mix again. Toss the salad while drizzling enough of the dressing over it to coat the leaves lightly. Add the croutons and toss again. Serve immediately, spooning the salad onto serving plates or passing the serving bowl around the table. Top each serving with anchovies, if using, or pass them separately.

SERVES 6 AS A FIRST COURSE OR 2 AS A MAIN COURSE

Perfect Croutons

You can make as few or as many of these as you have bread on hand. They keep well in a tightly sealed container at room temperature for 5 days, less if the weather is humid. The croutons add crunch and flavor to any salad or bowl of soup, especially creamy ones like the Butternut Squash Soup on page 86 or the Tomato Bisque on page 8.

Start with a not-too-dense loaf of Italian or French bread. The bread should be day-old or firm enough so that its crust is easy to remove and the bread itself can be cut into neat cubes. Cut the loaf into manageable lengths, stand each on its end, and shave off the crusts. Cut the bread into ½-inch cubes. Choose a mixing bowl that the bread cubes will fill no more than halfway. Pour olive oil into the palm of your hand, rub your hands together, then oil the sides of the bowl. Repeat until the bowl is lightly but completely greased. Add the bread cubes all at once and toss until they've absorbed the oil. The cubes should be lightly and evenly coated with oil. If not, oil your palms once or twice more and toss the bread again. If you like, sprinkle finely grated Parmesan cheese over the bread and toss again. Spread the seasoned bread out on a baking sheet. Do not overcrowd; if necessary, use more than one sheet. Bake in a 350°F oven for 5 minutes. Remove the baking sheet and stir the cubes gently, turning them and moving them around on the sheet. Bake 5 minutes and stir again. Continue baking until evenly golden brown, about 5 minutes. Remove and cool.

Main Courses and Side Dishes ◇

Poached Turkey Tonnato

Here is a simple—not to mention more economical—version of the classic Italian dish *vitello tonnato*, which is made by poaching a piece of veal, slicing it thinly, and saucing it with a tuna-and-caper-flavored mayonnaise. The sauce can be made ahead, but try to time things so the turkey is served at room temperature, not chilled. This version is, heresy of heresies, made with bottled mayonnaise. It is as wonderful as it is easy and impressive.

FOR THE TURKEY

One 2-pound boneless, skinless turkey breast
1 cup dry white wine
2 medium carrots, peeled and cut into ½-inch rounds
2 celery stalks, trimmed and cut into ½-inch pieces
1 yellow onion, cut into ½-inch slices
Salt
1 bay leaf

FOR THE MAYONNAISE

1 cup mayonnaise
Half 6-ounce can tuna packed in olive oil
1 tablespoon tiny (nonpareil) capers, plus more for the finished dish
5 anchovy fillets, or to taste
1 tablespoon fresh lemon juice, or as needed
Salt (optional)
Freshly ground black pepper
Chopped fresh Italian parsley

1. Put the turkey into a Dutch oven or flameproof casserole large enough to hold it comfortably. Pour in the wine and scatter the carrots, celery, and onion around the turkey. Pour in enough cold water to cover the turkey by 1 inch. Toss in a small handful of salt and the bay leaf. Bring to a boil over high heat, then adjust the heat so the liquid is at a bare simmer. Cook until no trace of pink remains at the center of the thickest part of the turkey (an instant-reading thermometer inserted into the center of the thickest part of the turkey breast will register 165°F), about 30 minutes. Remove from the heat and cool the turkey in the cooking liquid to room temperature.

2. Meanwhile, make the mayonnaise: Blend the mayonnaise, tuna, capers, anchovies (starting with fewer than 5 if you like), and lemon juice in a blender or food processor until the anchovies and capers are very finely chopped, not puréed. Scrape into a bowl and season with salt, if necessary, pepper, and additional lemon juice, if you like. The sauce should be thin enough to coat the back of a spoon heavily. If necessary, thin with the turkey cooking liquid, adding it a teaspoon at a time.

3. Remove the turkey from the cooking liquid and blot it dry. Slice the turkey on a 45-degree angle ½ inch thick. Arrange the slices, slightly overlapping, on a large serving platter. Spoon enough of the mayonnaise over the slices to coat them lightly but completely. Let stand at room temperature 30 minutes.

4. Just before serving, scatter additional capers and a little chopped parsley over the mayonnaise. Pass the remaining sauce separately.

THE TURKEY IS BEST IF SERVED WITHOUT REFRIGERATING. THE DISH CAN, HOWEVER, BE REFRIGERATED UP TO A DAY AFTER SLICING AND SAUCING. REFRIGERATE WITH A SHEET OF PLASTIC WRAP PRESSED DIRECTLY TO THE SURFACE OF THE SAUCE.

SERVES 4

Roast Turkey with Gravy

One 14- to 15-pound turkey, preferably fresh, or defrosted if frozen

1 teaspoon salt, plus more for seasoning the turkey

¼ teaspoon freshly ground black pepper, plus more for seasoning the turkey

2 medium carrots, peeled, trimmed, and cut into 1-inch lengths

2 medium yellow onions, unpeeled and cut into 8 wedges through the core

2 celery stalks, trimmed and cut into 2-inch lengths

6 tablespoons unsalted butter, softened

¼ cup lightly packed chopped fresh sage leaves

2 tablespoons packed fresh thyme leaves

4 cups Chicken Broth (page 37) or store-bought chicken broth

2 tablespoons cornstarch

1. Remove the neck and bag of giblets from the turkey cavity. Reserve the liver for another use or discard it. Rinse the turkey inside and out under cold running water. Drain as much of the water from the turkey as possible and pat the cavity dry with a paper towel. Season the cavity and skin generously with salt and pepper. Set the turkey in a roasting pan. Put a few pieces of each vegetable in the cavity and scatter the remaining vegetables around the turkey. Add the giblets and neck to the pan.

2. Combine the butter, sage, thyme, 1 teaspoon salt, and ¼ teaspoon pepper in a food processor. Process until the herbs are finely chopped. Starting at the neck end, work your hand between the skin and the breast meat to separate the skin from the meat. Work slowly and gently to separate the skin without tearing it. Work toward the thigh and continue separating the skin from the thighs. Rub the herb butter over the breast and thigh meat, spreading it evenly. Let the turkey stand at room temperature 30 minutes.

3. Meanwhile, place the rack in the center position and preheat the oven to 400°F. Roast the turkey until an instant-reading thermometer inserted into the thickest part of the thigh near the bone registers 165°F, about 2 hours and 15 minutes. Remove and let rest while preparing the gravy. If preparing the Traditional Corn Bread Dressing (page 29), put it in the oven now.

CONTINUED

4. With a thick wad of paper towels in each hand, tilt the turkey to drain off as much liquid from the cavity as possible. Lift the turkey to a carving board or platter. Add the broth to the roasting pan and place over high heat. Bring to a boil, stirring to remove the brown bits that stick to the pan. Strain the broth into a saucepan (ladle it in if the roasting pan is too hot or heavy to lift) and let stand several minutes until the fat rises to the top. Spoon off the fat.

5. Just before serving, bring the broth to simmering. Stir the cornstarch and ¼ cup water together in a small bowl until smooth. Stir the cornstarch mixture into the broth and simmer until thickened, 1 to 2 minutes. Cover and let stand while carving the turkey. Pour the gravy into a boat and pass separately.

SERVES 10, PLUS LEFTOVERS

Traditional Corn Bread Dressing

6 tablespoons unsalted butter, plus more for the cake pan

Buttermilk Corn Muffins (page 61)

1 cup chopped pecans, toasted (see tip for toasting walnuts on page 251)

1 medium yellow onion, cut into ¼-inch dice (about 1 ¼ cups)

1 celery stalk, trimmed and cut into ¼-inch dice (about ½ cup)

Salt

1 teaspoon dried thyme

½ teaspoon dried sage leaves

1 cup Chicken Broth (page 37) or store-bought chicken broth

Freshly ground black pepper

2 eggs, well beaten

1. Place a rack in the center position and preheat the oven to 400°F. Grease an 8-inch square cake pan with butter.

2. Prepare the corn muffin recipe and scrape it into the prepared pan. Bake until golden brown on top and the center springs back when gently pressed, about 25 minutes. Remove and cool 10 minutes. Remove the bread from the pan and cool completely. Wrap the corn bread in aluminum foil and store at room temperature up to 2 days. (In fact, it will be easier to crumble if it is not freshly baked.)

3. Crumble the corn bread coarsely into a large mixing bowl and add the pecans. Heat the butter in a large skillet over medium heat until foaming. Add the onion and celery. Season lightly with salt and cook, stirring, just until softened but not browned, about 5 minutes. Add the thyme and sage and cook 1 minute. Add the broth and bring to a simmer. Pour the contents of the skillet over the corn bread and toss well until mixed. Season with salt, if necessary, and pepper. Pour the eggs over the stuffing and mix well. Transfer the dressing to a lightly buttered 11-inch oval baking dish or any baking dish that fits the dressing comfortably. Cover with aluminum foil. The dressing can be made up to several hours in advance. Refrigerate until baking.

4. Preheat the oven to 400°F. Bake the dressing, still covered, 15 minutes (20 minutes if the dressing has been refrigerated). Uncover and continue baking until the top of the dressing is lightly browned and the dressing is heated through, about 15 minutes. Serve hot.

SERVES 10

Bree's Two-Step Braised Duck

One of Bree's favorite dishes, it should be prepared ahead of time so that the duck absorbs all the flavors. Bree is handy with a knife—particularly when it comes to cutting up the duck. She recommends a thin-bladed, just-sharpened 10-inch chef's knife, but if you prefer, just ask a butcher to do it for you.

One 5-pound duck, preferably fresh, or defrosted if frozen
2 medium carrots, peeled, trimmed, and cut into ¼-inch rounds
2 medium yellow onions, cut into ½-inch slices
2 tablespoons tomato paste
¼ cup Cognac or brandy
1 cup dry red wine
2 large rosemary sprigs
2 large thyme sprigs
2 large sage sprigs
1 bay leaf
2 tablespoons plain bread crumbs

STEP ONE

1. Preheat the oven to 450°F. Cut the duck into pieces: With kitchen shears cut the backbone from the duck, working steadily and carefully. Pull the wings and ends of the legs in opposite directions to separate the legs from the breasts, then cut off the legs with shears. Cut into the duck near where the wing attaches to the breast. Fish around a little to find the joint clearly and use the shears to remove the entire wing. Switch to a knife and cut the first (largest) joint from the wing. Cut the legs in half at the joint. Place the breast skin-side down and cut in half lengthwise along the breast bone. Cut each breast in half crosswise. Trim any overhanging fat from the leg and breast pieces and the first joint of the wing. These are the pieces that will end up in the stew. The rest of the wings, the backbone, neck, and giblets will be used to flavor the stew, then discarded.

2. Arrange the duck pieces, backbone, neck, and gizzards, skin-side up, in a roasting pan large enough to hold them comfortably. Scatter the carrots and onions around the duck. Roast 30 minutes. Turn the duck pieces, stir the vegetables, and continue roasting until well browned, 20 to 30 minutes.

CONTINUED

3. Working with heavy potholders, set the roasting pan over two burners. Remove all the duck pieces to a heavy pot or Dutch oven just large enough to hold them comfortably. Tilt the roasting pan to collect the fat in one corner. Spoon off as much of the fat as possible. Turn the burners under the roasting pan to medium. Add the tomato paste and cook, stirring, a minute or two, until the tomato paste changes color. Pour in the Cognac and cook until evaporated. Add the wine and bring to a boil, stirring to dissolve the tomato paste. Spoon the mixture into the pot with the duck. Pour in enough cold water to cover the duck. Add the rosemary, thyme, sage, and bay leaf. Bring to a boil over medium heat. Boil 2 minutes, spooning off the foam and fat that rises to the surface. Adjust the heat so the liquid is simmering. Cover and cook just until the duck pieces are tender when poked with a fork, about 40 minutes.

4. Remove the duck pieces with a slotted spoon, discarding the backbone, neck, gizzards, and two-piece wing tips as you go. Spread the remaining duck pieces on a plate and cool to room temperature. Cool the cooking liquid to room temperature. Cover and refrigerate the duck and liquid separately until the fat rises to the top and solidifies, at least 6 hours and up to 2 days.

STEP TWO

5. Remove the solid fat from the surface of the cooking liquid. Bring the liquid to a boil over high heat. Adjust the heat so the liquid is simmering. Stir in the bread crumbs and continue simmering until the sauce is reduced by about half and lightly thickened. Return the duck pieces to the sauce and cook, turning gently two or three times, until heated through. Serve hot, spooning some of the sauce over each serving.

SERVES 4

Bratwurst with Sweet-and-Sour Cabbage

3 tablespoons vegetable oil

8 small bratwurst or knockwurst (about 3 ounces each)

1 large yellow onion, thinly sliced (about 3 cups)

¼ cup white wine vinegar

2 tablespoons sugar

2 tablespoons gin (optional)

1 teaspoon salt

One 2-pound head red cabbage, dark leaves removed

1 tart apple, such as Granny Smith, peeled, cored, and cut into
½-inch dice

½ cup raisins

Freshly ground black pepper

VINEGAR, IN ADDITION TO ADDING FLAVOR AND SHARPNESS, WILL KEEP THE CABBAGE A CRISP PURPLISH-RED AND PREVENT IT FROM TURNING AN ODD BLUISH-GRAY.

1. Heat the oil in a large (about 11 x 3-inch-deep) heavy casserole over medium heat until rippling. Add the sausages and cook, turning, until browned on all sides, about 8 minutes. Transfer to a plate and set aside.

2. Add the onion and cook, stirring occasionally, until wilted and lightly browned, about 10 minutes.

3. Meanwhile, stir the vinegar, sugar, gin, if using, and salt together in a small bowl until the sugar is dissolved. Set aside. Cut the cabbage in quarters through the core. Cut out the core and cut the cabbage crosswise into ¼-inch strips. Toss the cabbage, apple, and raisins together in a bowl.

4. Pour the vinegar mixture into the onion. Cook, scraping the bottom until the vinegar comes to a boil and is reduced by half. Add about half the cabbage mixture and toss until the cabbage is coated with liquid. Continue adding more cabbage as room is made in the pan, until all the cabbage mixture is added.

5. Cover the pan, reduce the heat to medium-low, and cook, stirring occasionally, until the cabbage is very tender, about 20 minutes.

CONTINUED

6. Tuck the sausages into the cabbage and increase the heat to medium-high. Cook until almost all the liquid is evaporated and the sausages are heated through. Season to taste with pepper. Serve the sausages on individual plates on a bed of cabbage or make a bed of the cabbage on a large platter and top with the sausages.

SERVES 4

Chicken Cutlets Saltimbocca

The Italian word *saltimbocca* translates literally into the English phrase "jump in the mouth." Despite this fact, Bree still regards it as one of her favorite dishes. She knows better than to attach the sage leaves with toothpicks, which must then be plucked out after cooking. Instead, she hides the sage leaves under the prosciutto so they will stay in place on their own and will show up in silhouette after cooking. Sautéed spinach, tender green beans tossed in butter, or Buttery Baked Tomatoes (page 56) all make wonderful accompaniments.

Four 6- to 7-ounce boneless skinless chicken breasts
Salt and freshly ground black pepper
16 fresh sage leaves
4 slices prosciutto
3 tablespoons vegetable oil
All-purpose flour
¼ cup marsala or white wine
1 cup Chicken Broth (page 37) or store-bought chicken broth
2 tablespoons unsalted butter, cut into 8 small pieces

1. Cut each chicken breast crosswise into two more or less equal pieces. If the tenderloin—the little strip that runs along the underside of the breast—falls off, simply press it back on.

2. Tear off a 2-foot-long piece of plastic wrap and fold it in half crosswise to make a 12-inch square. Lay it flat on a sturdy surface and set two of the chicken pieces on the right hand side of the square, keeping a couple of inches between them. Fold the left side of the plastic wrap over the pieces to cover completely. Using the toothed side of a small meat mallet, pound the chicken pieces to an even ½-inch thickness. Don't worry if the chicken pieces take on an irregular shape. Repeat with the remaining chicken pieces. Season both sides of the chicken with salt and pepper.

3. Arrange two sage leaves over each piece of chicken and cover those with a half slice of prosciutto. Don't worry if the shape of the prosciutto doesn't exactly

CONTINUED

match the size of the chicken. Replace the plastic over the chicken and tap the prosciutto gently with the mallet to help the sage and prosciutto stick to the chicken. Transfer the chicken to a baking sheet. Repeat with the remaining chicken, sage, and prosciutto, replacing the plastic wrap as soon as it starts to fray. The chicken can be prepared to this point up to a few hours before cooking. Cover the baking sheet with plastic wrap and refrigerate.

4. Heat the oil in a heavy 12-inch skillet over medium-high heat until rippling. While it is heating, spread the flour out on a plate and coat half the cutlets with flour. Tap them gently to remove excess flour but leave the prosicutto and sage in place. Add the coated cutlets, prosciutto-side down, to the skillet and cook until golden brown. Flip the cutlets and cook the second side just until it loses its raw look and turns white, about 2 minutes. Remove the cutlets to a plate and coat and cook the remaining chicken.

5. Pour off the fat from the pan and return to the heat. Pour the marsala into the pan and bring to a boil while scraping the bottom of the pan with a wooden spoon to remove all the brown bits from the pan. When the marsala is almost evaporated, pour in the chicken broth. Bring to a boil and boil until the liquid is reduced by about half. Drop the butter pieces into the sauce and swirl the pan until the butter is melted. Return the cutlets to the sauce, overlapping them as necessary to make them fit. Continue boiling, spooning some of the sauce over the chicken, until the sauce is thick enough to lightly coat a spoon. Remove the pan from the heat and spoon 2 chicken pieces and some of the sauce onto each plate.

SERVES 4

Chicken Broth

Canned chicken broth will never enter the Van De Kamp home. In fact, it requires such minimal effort to make chicken broth at home that Bree thinks anyone who uses canned or dried chicken broth is nothing short of a barbarian. Or a Democrat. Either way, it's not a pretty picture to Bree.

3 pounds chicken backs, necks, and wings (any combination)
½ pound chicken gizzards
2 medium carrots, peeled and halved crosswise
1 celery stalk
1 medium yellow onion, skin left on, quartered

1. Rinse the chicken under cold running water and drain thoroughly. Put in a tall 8-quart pot along with the vegetables. Pour in enough water to cover by 2 inches and bring to a boil over high heat.

2. Adjust the heat to a gentle simmer. Skim any foam and fat from the surface. Simmer, skimming occasionally, 4 to 6 hours. If the water dips below the chicken and vegetables, replenish with more.

3. Pour or ladle the broth through a fine-mesh sieve into a bowl. Cool to room temperature, then refrigerate. Skim off and discard any fat that rises to the surface.

4. The broth may be refrigerated for up to 4 days or ladled into freezer containers and frozen for up to 3 months.

MAKES ABOUT 2 ½ QUARTS

Eve

Although not technically a housewife, the biblical Eve tops the list of *Desperate Housewives Throughout History* because of the obvious: She alone is responsible for Original Sin.

In the Book of Genesis, Eve gets Adam and herself thrown out of the Garden of Eden for eating the forbidden fruit of a certain tree. (Although this fruit is widely considered to be an apple, the Book of Genesis offers no more specifics than "fruit." Is it possible that Eve and Adam were ousted from the Garden for an orange, a pear, or even a mango? Nah. None of them quite have the *bite* of an apple.)

When you think about it, it is really not surprising that some form of food served as humankind's undoing. Even overlooking the fact that there are a staggering 311 references to the word *food* in the King James Version of the Bible (124 for fruit alone), it is obvious that foodstuffs—which provide nourishment, comfort, and pleasure—were very much on the minds of early men and women. Clearly, some things never change.

We all know the story. Satan, disguised as a serpent, seduces Eve into taking a bite of the fruit from the Tree of Knowledge of Good and Evil. The rest is history—literally. Eve takes a bite of the fruit and then convinces Adam to do the same. They are cast out of Paradise and into the flawed world we all know and love. After all, we wouldn't have *Desperate Housewives* without it.

Let's face it. We all give in to temptation. We want the one thing we are told we cannot have. Perhaps this is what makes us desperate. Whether it's fruit, a handsome plumber, or a promotion at the office, we've all found ourselves committing desperate acts.

Eve was just the first one to show us the way.

Fallen Apple Soufflé Cake

This is really a soufflé—coarsely puréed apples lightened with egg whites—that is baked, then allowed to fall, resulting in a cake that is moist and full of apple flavor. It is good warm or at room temperature, with or without ice cream or whipped cream.

6 tablespoons unsalted butter, plus more for the cake pan

⅓ cup granulated sugar, plus more for the baking dish

4 medium Golden Delicious apples (about 1½ pounds)

½ teaspoon ground cinnamon

2 large eggs, separated, plus 2 egg whites

½ cup plain dry bread crumbs

Confectioners' sugar

1. Preheat the oven to 400°F. Butter a 9-inch cake pan and sprinkle sugar over the sides and bottom to coat completely.

2. Cut the apples into quarters and cut out the cores and seeds. Peel the apples and cut them into rough ½-inch pieces. Melt the butter in a wide, heavy skillet over low heat. Add the apples and cinnamon. Cover and cook, stirring occasionally, until the apples are very tender when poked with a fork, about 30 minutes. Cool to room temperature.

3. Mash the cooled apples coarsely with a fork or potato masher. In a large bowl, beat ⅓ cup sugar and the egg yolks until they turn a lighter yellow. Stir in the mashed apples and the bread crumbs.

4. Beat the 4 egg whites in a separate bowl with a handheld mixer or whisk until the beaters leave soft peaks when lifted from the whites. With a rubber spatula, fold about ¼ of the egg whites into the apples to lighten the mixture, then fold in the remaining whites. Scrape the apple mixture into the prepared pan and bake until firm in the center and well browned, about 30 minutes. Cool, preferably on a wire rack, 15 minutes.

5. Invert the cake onto a serving plate. (If you like, invert the cake again so the browner, prettier side is facing up. This isn't terribly important, though, as the cake will be dusted with confectioners' sugar.) Let the cake cool to lukewarm or room temperature. Dust heavily with confectioners' sugar just before serving.

SERVES 8

Susan and Bree...

From: MayerArt@wisterialane.com
To: BVDK@wisterialane.com

Bree,
Wondering if I could bother you for the recipe for that amazing osso bucco you made the other night. I'm sure I'll find a way to ruin it no matter how much I follow your directions, but a girl's got to try!

By the way, was I dreaming or did I actually see you sleeping on your front lawn this morning? Get back to me when you can.

Susan!

Lamb Shanks Osso Bucco

There is a little surprise here, in the form of an optional hit of cinnamon, which backs up the rich, meaty taste of the lamb, mellowed with long cooking and pot vegetables. Either of the two serving suggestions found at the end of the recipe is suitable for even the swankiest gathering.

4 small lamb shanks (about 12 ounces each)
Kosher or sea salt and freshly ground black pepper
¼ cup vegetable oil
1 large onion, cut into ¼-inch dice (about 2 cups)
1 large carrot, peeled, trimmed, and cut into ¼-inch dice
    (about ¾ cup)
2 small celery stalks, trimmed and cut into ¼-inch dice
    (about ½ cup)
4 garlic cloves, coarsely chopped
1 cup dry red wine
1 ½ cups Chicken Broth (page 37) or store-bought chicken broth
2 fresh or dried bay leaves
1 cinnamon stick (optional)

1. Trim as much excess fat as possible from the shanks, but leave the outer membrane intact. It will hold the shanks together as they cook. Rub a generous amount of salt and pepper into all sides of the shanks.

2. Choose a heavy Dutch oven large enough to hold the shanks snugly in a single layer. Heat the oil in the pot over medium heat until rippling. Add the shanks and cook, turning as necessary, until browned on most sides. (Because of their shape, it won't be possible to brown the entire surface evenly.) If the fat begins to spatter, reduce the heat slightly. Transfer the shanks to a baking sheet and set aside.

3. Add the onion, carrot, celery, and garlic to the pot. Cook, stirring occasionally, until the vegetables pick up the browned bits stuck to the pan and start to brown further, about 6 minutes. Pour in the wine, bring to a boil, and cook until reduced by half. Pour in the chicken broth and add the bay leaves and cinnamon stick, if using. Return the shanks to the pot (the liquid will not cover them)

CONTINUED

and bring to a boil. Adjust the heat so the liquid is barely simmering and cover the pot. Cook, turning the shanks over every 30 minutes, until the meat is tender but not falling from the bone, about 2 hours. The shanks can be prepared to this point up to 2 days in advance. Cool to room temperature, then refrigerate, covered.

4. There are two ways to serve the shanks: in broth or in a lightly thickened sauce. For either, remove the shanks—carefully, to keep the meat from falling off the bone—to a platter or baking sheet. Pour or ladle the cooking liquid into a bowl. Wait several minutes, then skim the fat that rises to the surface. (If you've refrigerated the shanks, simply pull off the solidified fat from the surface before reheating.)

TO SERVE THE SHANKS IN BROTH:

Return the defatted cooking liquid to the pot and bring to a boil over high heat. Cook, stirring occasionally, until the liquid is reduced by about half; there should be about 2 cups. Return the shanks to the pot, reduce the heat to low, and cook the shanks, turning once, until thoroughly heated through. Serve each shank in a warmed shallow soup bowl and ladle some of the broth over each.

TO SERVE THE SHANKS IN A LIGHTLY THICKENED SAUCE:

Pass the defatted cooking liquid through a food mill fitted with the fine disc back into the pot. (If you don't have a food mill, the sauce can be made in a blender: Cool the sauce to room temperature first, then pulse in a blender, using very short on/off bursts just until the vegetables are very finely chopped. Don't overblend.) Bring to a boil over high heat. Reduce the heat to medium and cook until the liquid is reduced by about half. Return the shanks to the sauce and cook, turning once, until heated through. The shanks can be served in shallow bowls or on flat plates.

◄ ◄ WHETHER SERVING THE SHANKS IN BROTH OR LIGHTLY THICKENED SAUCE, POLENTA (PAGE 123), BUTTERED NOODLES, OR MASHED POTATOES ARE APPROPRIATE.

SERVES 4

Int. Van De Kamp House—Dining Room—Night

BREE:

So how's the Osso Bucco?

ANDREW (indifferent):

It's okay.

BREE:

It's okay. Andrew, I spent three hours cooking this meal. How do you think it makes me feel when you say "it's okay" in that sullen tone?

ANDREW:

Who asked you to spend three hours on dinner?

BREE:

Excuse me.

ANDREW:

Tim Harper's mom gets home from work, pops open a can of pork and beans, and boom! They're eating. Everyone's happy.

BREE:

You'd rather I serve pork and beans?

BREE stares COLDLY at her son. Beat.

DANIELLE:

Apologize now. I am begging.

ANDREW:

I'm saying do you always have to serve cuisine? Can't we ever just have food?

BREE:

Are you doing drugs?

Stuffed Cabbage

Heads of Savoy cabbage are looser than green cabbage, with crinkly dark to medium green leaves. They are easier to stuff than green cabbage, and better looking, too. After baking, the sauce is richly flavored and lightly thickened, perfect for spooning over a side of mashed potatoes.

1 medium head Savoy cabbage (about 2 pounds)

LEAVES FROM LOOSER HEADS— THOSE THAT GIVE A LITTLE WHEN SQUEEZED—WILL BE EASIER TO REMOVE.

FOR THE SAUCE

One 10 ¾-ounce can condensed tomato soup

1 cup store-bought beef broth

1 tablespoon light or dark brown sugar

1 tablespoon white wine vinegar

Freshly ground black pepper

FOR THE FILLING

1 pound ground beef

¼ cup uncooked long-grain rice

1 small onion, finely chopped

1 medium carrot, peeled, trimmed, and grated

1 teaspoon salt

½ teaspoon dried thyme

¼ teaspoon freshly ground black pepper

1. Heat a large pot of water to a boil. Meanwhile, separate 12 of the largest leaves from the head of cabbage by first cutting the stem of each leaf from the base, then gently pulling the leaf from the head. Cut out the thickest part of each leaf's stem (the bottom third or so). When the leaves are removed and stems trimmed, add them to the boiling water 2 or 3 at a time, submerging each batch before adding more. Cook 2 minutes after the water returns to a boil. Drain gently and cool.

2. Make the sauce: Measure out ¼ cup of the soup and set aside. Scrape the remaining soup into a small saucepan. Add the broth, brown sugar, and vinegar.

Bring to a boil, adjust the heat so the sauce is simmering, and cook, stirring occasionally, 10 minutes. Season to taste with pepper.

3. While the sauce is cooking, make the filling and stuff the cabbage leaves: Crumble the beef into a bowl. Add the rice, onion, carrot, salt, thyme, pepper, and reserved soup. Stir well or mix with your hands until all the ingredients are evenly distributed.

4. Heat the oven to 350°F. Spread a cabbage leaf out flat on the work surface. Overlap the edges where the stem was removed to make a neat, flat surface. Put about ⅓ cup of the beef filling (slightly less for smaller leaves, slightly more for larger leaves) on the bottom third of the leaf. Fold the bottom of the leaf over the filling, then fold the sides of the leaf over that. Roll into a compact cylinder. Repeat with the remaining leaves and filling. You may not fill all 12 leaves.

5. Spoon about ½ cup of the hot sauce over the bottom of an 8 x 11-inch baking dish. Set the cabbage rolls seam-side down and side by side into the dish. Spoon the remaining sauce over the rolls. Cover the dish tightly with aluminum foil and bake 1 ½ hours.

6. Uncover and continue baking until the leaves are very tender and the rice is fully cooked, about 30 minutes. Let stand 10 minutes before serving.

SERVES 4

Fillet of Red Snapper Livornese

Here is a simple, flavorful sauce that perks up fish. The sauce can be made well in advance of dinner and spooned over the fish right in the baking dish. Refrigerate and pull out to come to room temperature 30 minutes before baking. For 2 servings, simply divide the sauce ingredients in half and choose a smaller baking dish.

2 tablespoons olive oil, plus more for the baking dish

Four 7- to 8-ounce red snapper or grouper fillets, with skin on

Salt and freshly ground black pepper

1 small yellow onion, very finely chopped

2 garlic cloves, minced

2 ripe medium tomatoes, peeled, seeded, and diced (see box on page 48), about 1 cup, or 1 cup drained canned chopped tomatoes

¼ cup dry white wine

8 meaty black olives, pitted and coarsely chopped

1 tablespoon drained tiny (nonpareil) capers

2 tablespoons finely chopped fresh Italian parsley

1. Set a rack in the center position and preheat the oven to 400°F. Choose a baking dish that fits the fillets snugly. There should be very little room between the fillets or the fillets and the sides of the dish. Rub the dish with oil. Season the fillets well with salt and pepper.

2. Heat 2 tablespoons oil in a medium skillet over medium heat. Add the onion and garlic and cook, stirring often, until the onion is wilted, about 3 minutes. Add the tomatoes, wine, olives, capers, and ½ cup water and bring to a boil. Adjust the heat so the sauce is simmering. Cook 3 minutes. Stir in the parsley and salt and pepper to taste.

3. Spoon the sauce over and around the fish. Bake until the thickest part of the fillets is barely opaque, about 12 minutes. Serve directly from the dish.

SERVES 4

Flawlessly Peeled, Seeded, and Diced Tomatoes

Known as tomato concassée by Bree's culinary compatriots, peeled and diced tomatoes deliver the flavor of tomato without pesky seeds or skins. They are quite simple to make with any type of plum or round tomato.

Bring a large pot of water to a boil. Set a bowl of ice water next to the stove. Cut out the cores from the tomatoes and cut a small X in the end opposite the stem. Drop the tomatoes (no more than a few at a time) into the water and leave them just until the skin around the X begins to loosen, anywhere from 20 seconds for a very ripe tomato to a full minute for a less than perfectly ripe plum tomato. Scoop them out with a slotted spoon and immerse them in ice water. When chilled, peel off the skin and cut them in half—lengthwise for plum tomatoes, along the "equator" for round tomatoes. Squeeze and/or spoon out the seeds and liquid. Cut the flesh into neat dice.

Lobster Risotto with Herb Oil

This ultrachic, no-holds-barred main course also makes a wonderful side dish or opener for a fancy dinner party.

Salt

One 1½-pound live lobster

6 tablespoons olive oil

12 chives

Leaves from 3 large thyme sprigs

1 small yellow onion, very finely chopped (about ¾ cup)

1 small leek, cleaned (see page 5) and very finely chopped (about 1 cup)

1 ½ cups Italian arborio rice (see Note on page 51)

½ cup Prosecco (dry Italian sparkling wine) or other dry sparkling wine

4 cups hot Chicken Broth (page 37) or store-bought chicken broth

1 ripe medium tomato, peeled, seeded, and chopped (see box opposite), optional

2 tablespoons chopped fresh Italian parsley

2 tablespoons unsalted butter, cut into small pieces (optional)

1. Heat a large pot of water to a boil. Throw in a handful of salt. Slip the lobster into the water, partially cover the pot, and cook 8 minutes from the time the water returns to a boil. Remove the lobster and let it stand until cool enough to handle. Twist the tail to separate it from the body. Cut through the underside of the tail with a pair of shears and pull out the tail in one piece. Use a sturdy pair of nutcrackers to crack the claws and the two "knuckles" attached to them. Remove the meat from the claws and knuckles. Cut all the lobster meat into ½-inch pieces.

2. Make the herb oil: Combine ¼ cup of the olive oil, the chives, and the thyme leaves in a food processor. Blend until the oil is a vivid green. Strain into a small bowl and set aside. (The herb oil and lobster can be prepared up to a day in advance. Cover and refrigerate both.)

IF YOU'RE FEELING AMBITIOUS AND ARE PREPARING THE HERB OIL AND LOBSTER A DAY IN ADVANCE, TRY THIS SIMPLE FLAVOR BOOSTER: COMBINE ALL THE LOBSTER SHELLS AND THE BROTH CALLED FOR IN THE INGREDIENTS IN A MEDIUM SAUCEPAN. BRING TO A BOIL, ADJUST THE HEAT SO THE LIQUID IS SIMMERING, AND COVER THE POT. COOK 20 MINUTES AND STRAIN. REFRIGERATE THE BROTH UNTIL NEEDED AND USE IN PLACE OF THE PLAIN CHICKEN BROTH CALLED FOR IN THE RECIPE.

CONTINUED

3. About 35 minutes before serving, heat the remaining 2 tablespoons oil in a 4- to 5-quart pot over medium heat. Add the onion and leek and cook, stirring, until tender and just lightly browned, about 8 minutes. Stir in the rice and cook, stirring, until the edges turn white and the center chalky, about 2 minutes. Pour in the wine and cook, stirring and scraping the bottom, until evaporated.

4. Add enough of the hot stock to cover the rice. Adjust the heat so the broth is at a lively simmer. Cook, stirring, until almost all of the broth is absorbed. Continue adding enough broth to cover the rice and stirring until absorbed, until the rice is tender but firm and there is enough liquid to make a creamy sauce for the rice, about 15 minutes. You may use slightly more or less than 4 cups of broth, depending on the rice, technique, and the shape of the pot. The consistency of the finished rice can be adjusted at the end by adding a little liquid for a creamier rice or by cooking for a minute or two for a denser rice. Stir in the lobster, tomato, parsley, and butter, if using. Ladle into warm shallow bowls and drizzle some of the herb oil over each. Serve immediately.

SERVES 3 TO 4 AS A MAIN COURSE
OR 8 AS A SIDE DISH OR FIRST COURSE

Note: Arborio rice is a medium-grain rice that is quite different from long-grain (i.e., Carolina) rice. It is available in gourmet supermarkets, specialty stores, and online (see Sources, page 266).

Rocky Road Sweet Potatoes

Salt
3 large orange-fleshed sweet potatoes (about 3 pounds)
1 cup mini marshmallows
½ cup toasted chopped pecans (see tip for walnut toasting on page 251)
2 tablespoons unsalted butter
¼ cup pure maple syrup
2 tablespoons orange juice

1. Throw a handful of salt into a large pot of water. Peel the sweet potatoes and cut them into rough 2-inch chunks, dropping them into the salted water as you go. Bring to a boil over high heat. Lower the heat to medium and cook until the sweet potatoes are tender but still intact, about 20 minutes. Drain the sweet potatoes and rinse them briefly under cold water. Drain thoroughly and put into an 11 x 9-inch baking dish. Scatter the marshmallows and pecans evenly over the top of the sweet potatoes.

2. Bring the butter, maple syrup, and orange juice to a boil in a small saucepan. Dip a potato masher in the maple syrup mixture (to keep it from sticking) and mash the sweet potatoes very coarsely, incorporating the marshmallows and pecans into the sweet potatoes. Pour the maple syrup mixture over the sweet potatoes. Cover the dish with aluminum foil. Bake now or refrigerate for up to 1 day.

3. To bake: Preheat the oven to 350° F. Bake, covered, 20 minutes (30 minutes for sweet potatoes that have been refrigerated). Uncover and continue baking until the potatoes are browned and the pan juices are bubbling. Serve hot.

TO MAKE INDIVIDUAL SERVINGS:

Drain the sweet potatoes and transfer them to a large mixing bowl. Top with the marshmallows and pecans. Using a potato masher, mash the potatoes coarsely, incorporating the pecans and marshmallows as you do. Divide the mixture among eight 8-ounce baking cups or ramekins. Make the orange juice glaze as described above and pour it over the sweet potatoes in the cups, dividing it evenly. Place the cups in a baking pan large enough to hold them snugly and bake them as described above.

SERVES 8

Steamed Tiny Potatoes with Herb Butter

This method works well for small potatoes—whether red or white "new" potatoes—or even some of the varieties that have become more and more available, like purple potatoes, yellow Finns, or fingerlings. Whatever the variety, the thinner the skins, the better this technique will work.

1 pound tiny potatoes of any variety (no more than ¾ inch across
   at the widest point)
Salt and freshly ground black pepper
2 tablespoons unsalted butter, cut into small pieces
¼ cup loosely packed, coarsely chopped fresh dill or 2 tablespoons
   finely chopped fresh chives

1. Wash the potatoes well. Put them into a heavy shallow pan or flameproof casserole into which they fit comfortably in a single layer. Pour in ¼ inch of water. Season lightly with salt and pepper and scatter the butter pieces over the potatoes. Bring the liquid in the pan to a simmer over medium-low heat. Cover tightly and cook until the potatoes are tender when poked with the tip of a paring knife, 15 to 20 minutes, depending on the type of potato. Check once or twice to make sure there is at least a thin layer of water in the pot.

2. Uncover the pot, increase the heat to medium-high, and cook until the water is evaporated and the potatoes begin to sputter. Scatter the herb of choice over the potatoes and wiggle the pot by the handles to roll the potatoes in the herb butter. Check the seasoning and add salt and/or pepper as needed. Serve hot.

SERVES 4

Ginger-Spiked Baby Carrots

¼ cup Chicken Broth (page 37) or store-bought chicken broth

1 tablespoon soy sauce

2 teaspoons sugar

½ teaspoon ground cumin

¼ teaspoon dried ginger

One 1-pound bag baby carrots

2 tablespoons unsalted butter, cut into small pieces

1. Stir the broth, soy sauce, sugar, cumin, and ginger together in a deep 11-inch skillet or casserole until the sugar is dissolved. Add the carrots and toss to coat with seasoning. Dot with the butter. Bring to a boil over medium heat. Adjust the heat so the liquid is at a steady simmer. Cover tightly and cook until the carrots are tender but still firm, about 20 minutes.

2. Uncover, increase the heat, and boil until the carrots are lightly coated with glaze, about 2 minutes. Serve hot or at room temperature.

SERVES 4

Buttery Baked Tomatoes

When you think tomatoes, you probably think Mediterranean and olive oil. Switch tracks and try these delicious, meltingly tender baked tomatoes made rich with a touch of butter. Multiply the proportions below as needed for a larger group.

2 ripe medium plum tomatoes (about ½ pound)
Salt and freshly ground black pepper
1 tablespoon unsalted butter
2 tablespoons fine dry bread crumbs
½ teaspoon dried thyme or oregano

1. Place a rack in the center position and preheat the oven to 375°F.

2. Core the tomatoes and cut them in half lengthwise. Squeeze out most of the seeds and liquid. Flick out the remaining seeds with the tip of a knife. Arrange the tomatoes, cut-side up, in a small baking dish. Season the insides well with salt and pepper.

3. Melt the butter in a small skillet. Stir in the bread crumbs and herb of choice. Top the tomatoes with the seasoned bread crumbs, dividing them evenly. Bake until the crumb topping is golden brown and the tomatoes are tender, about 25 minutes. The tomatoes may be served hot but are better at room temperature.

SERVES 2

Buckwheat Pancakes

FOR THE BUCKWHEAT PANCAKE MIX

(MAKES 2 ½ CUPS; CAN BE MULTIPLIED UP TO 4 TIMES)

> 1 ½ cups all-purpose flour
>
> 1 cup buckwheat flour
>
> ¼ cup sugar
>
> 2 ½ teaspoons baking powder
>
> ½ teaspoon salt

FOR EACH BATCH

> 2 cups milk
>
> 4 tablespoons (¼ cup) unsalted butter, melted, or ¼ cup vegetable oil,
>   plus more for cooking the pancakes
>
> 1 large egg
>
> 1 recipe (2 ½ cups) Buckwheat Pancake Mix (above)
>
> Softened butter
>
> Warm maple syrup

1. Stir the flours, sugar, baking powder, and salt together in a mixing bowl. If making a single batch, proceed to the next step. If making a multiple batch of dry ingredients, transfer the mix to a tightly sealed container and store in a dark, dry place.

2. Beat the milk, ¼ cup butter, and egg together in a large mixing bowl. If necessary, measure out 2 ½ cups of the mix. Add to the milk mixture and stir just until blended. Don't overmix; some lumps are fine. Let stand 10 minutes.

CONTINUED

3. Heat a griddle or large pan over medium heat until a few drops of water flicked onto the surface dance for a second or two before evaporating. If the water evaporates immediately, the pan is too hot. If it takes longer than 2 seconds to evaporate, the pan is too cold. Adjust the heat accordingly. Grease the griddle or pan. Using ⅔ cup batter for each, pour the batter onto the griddle to make 5- to 6-inch pancakes. Cook until the underside is golden brown and lacy, about 4 minutes. Flip the pancakes and cook until the second side is golden brown in spots, about 3 minutes. Serve immediately, slathered with additional butter and maple syrup.

MAKES SIX THICK 6-INCH PANCAKES

Blueberry Muffins

Vegetable oil cooking spray
12 tablespoons (1 ½ sticks) unsalted butter, cut into 8 pieces
1 ½ cups milk
3 large eggs
Grated zest of 1 orange
3 cups all-purpose flour, preferably bleached
⅔ cup sugar, plus more for sprinkling on the tops of the muffins
1 tablespoon baking powder
¾ teaspoon salt
¼ teaspoon nutmeg, preferably freshly grated
1 ½ cups fresh blueberries, frozen, or 1 ½ cups frozen blueberries
   (see Note)

1. Place a rack in the center position and preheat the oven to 400°F. Spray a 12-compartment muffin tin (see page 60) with vegetable oil cooking spray.

2. Combine the butter and milk in a small saucepan over very low heat. When the butter is half melted, pour the mixture into a small mixing bowl and stir until the butter is completely melted. Whisk in the eggs and orange zest thoroughly and set aside.

3. Stir the flour, ⅔ cup sugar, baking powder, salt, and nutmeg together in a large bowl. Add the berries and toss to coat with flour. Pour the milk mixture over the dry ingredients and stir gently from the bottom up just until no white streaks remain. The batter will look lumpy.

4. Divide the batter among the muffin tin compartments. There will be enough batter to fill each compartment to just below the rim. Sprinkle the top of each muffin evenly with sugar. Bake until golden brown and a toothpick inserted into the center of a muffin comes out clean, about 22 minutes.

5. Cool the muffins in the tin on a wire rack for 10 minutes. Remove from the tins and cool completely before serving.

MAKES 12 MUFFINS

Note: When fresh or defrosted, blueberries tend to streak the batter and turn it a nasty bluish-green. Frozen blueberries stay intact and remain juicy. Look for small frozen blueberries or, better yet, buy small fresh berries in season and freeze them yourself: Spread the berries out in a single layer on a paper towel–lined baking sheet and place in a level spot in the freezer. Freeze until solid, about an hour, then transfer to sealable freezer bags.

About These Muffins

- Enormous, supersweet, greasy muffins are not Bree's cup of tea. These three recipes make moist, delicate 3-inch-or-so muffins, using a 12-compartment tin with 2¾ x 1¼-inch compartments. If your tins have smaller or larger compartments, adjust the baking time as necessary.

- When folding the dry and wet ingredients together, use a large rubber spatula to scrape the bottom of the bowl and bring the batter up and over the ingredients on top. Use as few strokes as needed to just moisten the dry ingredients. Overmixing will make rubbery, dry muffins.

- Muffins are best when eaten within several hours of baking. Day-old muffins, however, are wonderful when split in half and toasted, either healthfully (under a broiler or in a toaster oven) or sinfully (each half slathered with butter and cooked, butter-side down, in a heavy skillet or on a griddle).

Buttermilk Corn Muffins

These are equally at home at the breakfast or dinner table. For breakfast, try them with maple syrup and butter. For dinner, they are neat accompaniments to chilis, stews, or barbecued ribs, especially in their chili and/or cheese incarnations. (See Variations on page 62.)

Vegetable oil cooking spray
1 ⅓ cups buttermilk
6 tablespoons unsalted butter, melted
2 large eggs
1 ½ cups fine yellow cornmeal
1 cup all-purpose flour
¼ cup sugar
2 teaspoons baking powder
1 teaspoon salt
½ teaspoon baking soda

1. Place a rack in the center position and preheat the oven to 400°F. Spray a 12-compartment muffin tin (see opposite page) with vegetable oil cooking spray.

2. Combine the buttermilk and butter in a small saucepan over very low heat. When the butter is half melted, pour the mixture into a small mixing bowl and stir until the butter is completely melted. Whisk in the eggs thoroughly and set aside.

3. Stir the cornmeal, flour, sugar, baking powder, salt, and baking soda together in a large bowl. Pour the milk mixture over the dry ingredients and stir gently from the bottom up just until no white streaks remain. The batter will look lumpy.

4. Divide the batter among the muffin tin compartments. There will be enough batter to fill each compartment about three quarters. Bake until the tops are lightly browned and a toothpick inserted into the center of a muffin comes out clean, about 16 minutes.

5. Cool the muffins in the tin on a wire rack for 10 minutes. Remove from the tins and cool completely before serving.

MAKES 12 MUFFINS

Add ½ cup finely shredded sharp Cheddar and/or 1 jalapeño pepper, split in half lengthwise, seeded, and finely chopped, to the dry ingredients.

Pineapple Bran Muffins

Bran muffins can give healthy breakfasts a bad name. In these, the pineapple keeps the muffins moist and adds a mysterious flavor. They are wonderful split, toasted, and spread with orange marmalade.

Vegetable oil cooking spray
One 20-ounce can crushed pineapple in juice
1 ½ cups coarse wheat bran
1 ¼ cups all-purpose flour
½ cup light brown sugar
¼ cup whole wheat flour
2 teaspoons baking powder
½ teaspoon baking soda
½ teaspoon salt
¼ teaspoon ground cinnamon
¼ cup ground allspice (optional)
1 cup milk
½ cup vegetable oil
¼ cup molasses
2 eggs

1. Place a rack in the center position and preheat the oven to 400°F. Spray a 12-compartment muffin tin (see page 60) with vegetable oil cooking spray.

2. Drain the pineapple in a fine-mesh sieve over a bowl. Press the pineapple with a spoon to extract as much of the liquid as possible. Set the pineapple aside and reserve the juice for another use, like the Pineapple-Peach Smoothie on page 171.

3. Stir the bran, all-purpose flour, brown sugar, whole wheat flour, baking powder, baking soda, salt, cinnamon, and allspice, if using, together in a large bowl. Rub the dry ingredients between your palms to crumble the brown sugar thoroughly and to distribute all ingredients evenly.

4. In a separate bowl, whisk together the milk, vegetable oil, molasses, eggs, and drained pineapple. Pour the egg mixture over the dry ingredients and stir gently from the bottom up just until no dry streaks remain. The batter will look lumpy.

CONTINUED

5. Divide the batter among the muffin tin compartments. There will be enough batter to fill each compartment. Bake until the tops are lightly browned and a toothpick inserted into the center of a muffin comes out clean, about 20 minutes. Cool the muffins in the tin on a wire rack for 10 minutes. Remove from the tins and cool completely before serving.

MAKES 12 MUFFINS

Bree Van De Kamp
cordially invites you to her home at

19 Wisteria Lane
on Sunday, September 24th
Cocktails at 6:00 P.M.

Dinner will be served promptly at 7:00 P.M.

Dress: Cocktail Dresses for Women
Jackets and Ties for Men Required

R.S.V.P. by September 17th

Desserts ◇

Steamed Christmas Pudding, Brandy Flambé

This is somewhat lighter—in color and texture—than a traditional steamed pudding. After a few weeks soaking with rum, the pudding doesn't require much additional rum to flambé, so be prudent with the alcohol.

1 cup raisins

20 dried apricots, cut into ½-inch dice (about 1 cup)

¼ pound pitted dates, cut into ½-inch dice (about ⅔ cup)

¼ cup dark rum or brandy, plus more for soaking the finished pudding if you like

1 stick (8 tablespoons) unsalted butter, at room temperature, plus more for greasing the dish

1 cup all-purpose flour

½ teaspoon baking powder

1 teaspoon dried ginger

½ teaspoon ground cinnamon

¼ teaspoon ground allspice

½ cup brown sugar

Grated zest of 1 lemon

3 large eggs

2 cups coarse pound cake crumbs (made from semistale pound cake)

1 cup milk

1. Toss the dried fruit and ¼ cup rum together in a medium bowl, breaking up any fruit that sticks together. Let stand, tossing two or three times, 30 minutes.

2. Generously butter a 6-cup soufflé dish. For steaming the pudding, choose a heavy pot wide enough so the pudding can be put into and taken out of it easily. The pot must be deep enough to hold the pudding when covered. Pour 1 inch of water into the pot and find something that will hold the pudding about

CONTINUED

1 inch from the bottom of the pot during cooking. Small metal trivets made for this purpose are sold in cookware stores, but you can improvise with two overturned custard cups, a round cooling rack, or any other heat- and waterproof items that will do the trick.

3. Stir the flour, baking powder, and spices together in a separate bowl and set aside. Beat 8 tablespoons butter, the sugar, and the lemon zest until smooth. Beat in the eggs one at a time, beating well after each. Fold in the soaked fruits and any rum left in the bowl. Fold in the cake crumbs, then the flour mixture. Pour in the milk and stir just until evenly blended. Scrape into the prepared soufflé dish. Cover tightly with aluminum foil.

4. Heat the water in the pot to boiling. Adjust the heat so the water is at a steady, gentle boil. Put the pudding on the rack or trivets, cover the pot, and steam until evenly cooked through and slightly risen in the center, about 3 hours. Check the water from time to time and replenish if necessary.

5. Remove the pudding and cool to room temperature. Invert the pudding onto a plate. The pudding can be served right away or refrigerated for up to 3 weeks. If refrigerating, return the pudding to the soufflé dish. Pour about 2 tablespoons of rum onto the pudding every other day until serving. The pudding will soak up just about as much rum as you can pour onto it. To flambé, bring the pudding to room temperature at least 2 hours before serving, if necessary. Pour 2 to 3 tablespoons of rum onto the pudding and ignite the rum with a long match. Serve as soon as the flames die down.

SERVES 12

White chocolate is *not* actually chocolate. In fact, the popular sweet does not contain a single drop of the genuine article. It is made of cocoa butter, which gives it its "chocolaty" flavor. The cocoa butter is blended with milk and sugar to form the creamy confection, which is used for both eating and cooking.

Bree offers that you can certainly use white chocolate in certain dishes, but "don't pretend you're using chocolate."

Blueberry Crisp

The topping here calls for pine nuts, but you can substitute any soft, oily nut, like walnuts or pecans.

FOR THE TOPPING

½ cup pine nuts

⅔ cup all-purpose flour

⅓ cup light brown sugar

⅓ cup granulated sugar

6 tablespoons room-temperature unsalted butter, cut into 6 pieces

FOR THE BERRIES

½ cup granulated sugar

1 tablespoon cornstarch

Finely grated zest of 1 orange

¼ teaspoon ground ginger or cinnamon

3 pints blueberries, rinsed and thoroughly drained

3 tablespoons unsalted butter, cut into small pieces

1. Preheat the oven to 350°F.

2. Spread the pine nuts out on a baking sheet and bake until very lightly browned, about 8 minutes. Stir the nuts on the sheet once or twice as they cook so they brown evenly. Cool them completely.

3. While the pine nuts are cooling, make the berry filling: Stir ½ cup granulated sugar, the cornstarch, orange zest, and ginger together in a large bowl until blended. Add the blueberries and toss gently. Let stand, tossing gently occasionally, until the blueberries start to get juicy. Scrape the berries into an 11-inch oval baking dish. Dot the top with the butter.

4. Make the topping: Stir the flour, brown sugar, and ⅓ cup granulated sugar together in a small bowl until blended. Add the 6 tablespoons room-temperature butter and cooled pine nuts and rub the ingredients together with your fingertips until the butter is completely absorbed by the flour and sugar. (It is fine if some of the pine nuts are broken up and some are whole.) Sprinkle the topping evenly over the berries and bake until the topping is lightly browned and the berries are bubbling and lightly thickened, about 40 minutes. Remove and cool at least 45 minutes before serving.

SERVES 8

Susan

Perennial good girl Susan

Mayer has a thing for kitchens. She loves spending count-less hours in them. In fact, she loves everything about them. The thing is, the kitchens don't seem to reciprocate the feeling. In fact, the more time Susan spends in them, the less they seem to be kind to her.

Ever since she was a little girl, Susan's had a tough time in that particular section of the house. Susan pictured herself maturing into a full-blossomed wife and mother like Donna Reed—television's perfect wife and mother. As the years passed and she was ready to go to college, Susan began to be more realistic about expectations.

When Karl was courting Susan, she insisted that he come over for dinner to try her cooking. Luckily, Karl was smitten anyway.

When she and Karl were starting their lives together, the one thing Susan wanted to master was an excellent cup of coffee. After all, she knew that she needed to be able to offer something to people who stopped by. And although it wasn't much, she thought maybe she could be known for her stellar cappuccino. In fact, she grew to like the idea of being "Susan, who makes that really great cup of coffee." She bought unusual, interesting cups and saucers. She stocked her pantry with some exotic coffee cookies to keep on hand for company. Truth is, she pulled it off. Susan actually made a great cup of coffee. Unfortunately, it tended to follow a rather "lackluster" meal, which was Karl's nice way of describing something barely fit for human con-sumption. And even worse, Susan had somehow found a way to ruin the expensive after-dinner cookies, too.

Unfortunately, Susan's marriage didn't work out, but it nonetheless gave her the most important gift of her life: her intelligent, mature, and self-possessed daughter, Julie. It was as if Julie was the manifestation of all the things Susan wanted to be when she grew up and became an adult. Julie was even learning how to cook. Clearly, Susan was doing something right.

Over the years, Susan has kept the belief that she will eventually crack one of these recipes. She hopes one day there will be a dish that will come out well *every* time she makes it. But she realizes that her culinary dreams are still a ways in the distance.

A woman with better intentions than kitchen skills, Susan believes that it's the thought that counts. But the road to hell is paved with the best intentions, and the road to gastrointestinal illness often starts in Susan Mayer's kitchen.

Recipes in this chapter are "Susan-proof"; for the most part, ingredients are plunked into a skillet, baking dish, or fondue pot and heat does the rest. All that is required is to follow the instructions. The truth is, although many of us wish we were like Bree in the kitchen, in reality, we're far more like Susan. And that should be a comforting thought while preparing the following dishes.

Susan's entire marriage to Karl can be traced through one particular dish: macaroni and cheese.

It was too salty the night she and Karl moved into the house.

It was too watery the night she found lipstick on Karl's shirt.

She burned it the night Karl told her he was leaving her for his secretary.

Margaritas

2 cups good-quality Mexican tequila
1 cup Cointreau, good-quality curaçao, or other orange liqueur
½ cup freshly squeezed lime juice
Kosher salt
Coarsely cracked ice
Thin lime wedges (optional)

1. Stir the tequila, Cointreau, and lime juice together in a pitcher. Refrigerate for up to a day if you like.

2. When ready to serve the drinks, fold a sheet of paper towel into quarters. Place on a small plate and soak thoroughly with water. Spread out a thick layer of kosher salt on a second plate. Wet the rims of cocktail glasses by pressing them into the wet paper towel, then line the rims with salt by pressing them lightly into the salt. Stand them upright.

3. Pour about ½ cup margarita mix for each drink into a tall cocktail shaker half-filled with cracked ice. Close the shaker and shake vigorously. Strain into the prepared glasses. Drop a lime wedge into each glass if you like.

MAKES EIGHT 4-OUNCE DRINKS
(CAN BE EASILY DOUBLED OR HALVED)

Note: The choice of tequila is a personal one. Some people don't mind ordinary brand-name tequilas; others seek out Añejo (old) or reposada (aged) tequilas with more character and depth of flavor.

Susan on dreams . . .

Having once taken a class on dream interpretation, Susan discovered that when you have a dream about cooking, it means that a pleasant duty will befall you. Many friends will come for a visit in the near future.

That night Susan had a dream that her friends came over for dinner. Unfortunately, Susan is as ill-equipped when it comes to cooking in her dreams as she is in reality. Waking up in a cold sweat, Susan vowed one thing: She would never take a class on dream interpretation again.

◄◄ *Susan's Margaritas at left, a dream come true.*

Traditional Cheese Fondue

Ultraprocessed "Swiss" cheese just won't cut it here. A trip to a gourmet market or cheese shop to get the real articles pays off in rich flavor and a supersmooth consistency.

1 garlic clove, cut in half
1 cup Swiss Neuchâtel or Apremont wine, dry Riesling,
  or other fruity but dry white wine, or as needed
1 ½ cups coarsely grated Gruyère cheese (about 5 ounces)
1 ½ cups coarsely grated Emmenthaler cheese (about 5 ounces)
2 teaspoons cornstarch
1 tablespoon kirsch or other clear fruit brandy
Freshly ground black pepper
1 loaf crusty baguette, cut into 1-inch cubes

1. Rub the inside of a fondue pot or heavy earthenware casserole with the garlic, then discard the clove. Pour in 1 cup of wine and heat over medium-low heat until the wine is steaming and just about to simmer. Do not boil. Stir in the cheese one handful at a time, waiting for each to be completely melted before adding another. (The cheese and wine may stay separate at this point; that is fine.) Adjust the heat as necessary to keep the fondue just below the boiling point. When all the cheese is added and melted, stir the cornstarch and kirsch together in a small bowl, then stir that mixture into the pot. Stir until smooth and creamy. If, after adding the cornstarch mixture, the fondue still isn't smooth, switch to a wire whisk and whisk gently until smooth. Season to taste with pepper.

2. Bring the pot to the table set over a very low heat, such as a votive candle (or use the setup that comes with the fondue pot). Put the bread cubes in a basket and use fondue forks to spear them and dunk them in the cheese. Keep some wine at hand and use it to thin the fondue if it becomes too thick for easy dunking.

SERVES 6

Spiced Shrimp in the Shell

Although Susan has accidentally eaten the shell (on too many occasions to bother mentioning), she still has a fondness for this summertime meal that is less labor-intensive than most recipes and therefore less likely to be ruined than most.

IN A PINCH, SUB-
STITUTE ¼ CUP
OLD BAY SEA-
SONING FOR THE
SALT, CELERY,
MUSTARD, PEP-
PERCORNS,
CLOVES, AND
CAYENNE.

1 small yellow onion, cut in quarters through the core

1 lemon, cut into wedges

10 garlic cloves

¼ cup salt

1 tablespoon celery seeds

1 tablespoon mustard seeds (optional)

2 teaspoons whole peppercorns

1 teaspoon whole cloves

½ teaspoon cayenne pepper

2 pounds large shrimp (21 to 25 per pound)

1. Put all the ingredients except the shrimp in a 4-quart pot. Pour in 2 quarts of water. Bring to a boil and cover. Cook 10 minutes.

2. Add the shrimp and remove from the heat. Let steep 4 minutes. Drain immediately and transfer to a serving bowl. Serve hot or at room temperature.

SERVES 8 AS A FIRST COURSE
OR 4 AS A MAIN COURSE

Roasted Peppers and Fresh Mozzarella Topped with Arugula Salad

2 large red bell peppers (about 1 ¼ pounds)

½ pound fresh mozzarella, preferably salted

Coarse salt (sea, kosher, or other) and coarsely cracked black pepper

1 bunch small, tender arugula, thick stems removed, washed and dried (about 4 cups)

3 tablespoons extra-virgin olive oil

Salt and freshly ground black pepper

Balsamic vinegar (if you must)

1. Roast and peel the peppers (see page 83) and tear them into strips about 1 ½ inches wide. Slice the mozzarella a scant ½ inch thick. Overlap the pepper strips and mozzarella slices on a plate large enough to hold them comfortably. Season to taste with coarse salt and cracked black pepper and let stand at room temperature about 30 minutes.

2. Just before serving, toss the arugula with the olive oil. Season lightly with salt and pepper and toss again. If you feel lost without it, drizzle a small amount of balsamic vinegar over the salad and toss again. Mound the arugula over the mozzarella and peppers, scraping all of the oil from the bowl. Let stand 3 to 4 minutes so the dressing will drip from the arugula onto the mozzarella and peppers. Scoop some of each ingredient onto the serving plates.

SERVES 2 AS A MAIN COURSE
OR 4 AS A SALAD

Roasted Peppers

Roasting peppers—red, yellow, or green bell peppers or hot chili peppers like jalapeños or poblanos—intensifies their flavor and softens their texture. Whichever type of pepper you pick, the methods for roasting and peeling them are basically the same.

Stovetop (not recommended for small chilies like jalapeños or serranos): Turn the burner(s) to high. Set the peppers on the grate directly over the flames. Turn as necessary with a pair of long tongs until the skin is blackened on all sides. Prop the peppers at different angles on the burner grate to reach all the crevices.

Broiler: Place the oven rack about 6 inches from the broiler (an inch or two closer for small chilies) and preheat the broiler to high. Place the peppers on a broiler pan and broil, turning as necessary with a pair of long tongs, until charred on all sides.

After roasting, put the peppers in a bowl, cover the bowl with plastic wrap, and cool the peppers completely. With your hands, rub as much of the blackened skin off the peppers as you can, then cut the pepper in half (or pull bell peppers apart along their natural creases). Be careful: The liquid inside large bell peppers can stay quite hot after the outside of the pepper has cooled. Scrape the cores, ribs, seeds, and any remaining blackened skin from the peppers with a knife. The peppers are now ready to use.

Chipotle-Glazed Chicken Wings

C hipotles are jalapeño chilies that have been smoked and dried. They are available loose (these need soaking before using) or simmered in a well-seasoned tomato sauce (known as adobo) and packed into small cans.

2 pounds largish chicken wings (8 whole wings)
1 teaspoon salt
¼ teaspoon freshly ground black pepper
¼ cup adobo sauce from canned chipotles or chipotle adobo sauce
   (see Sources, page 266)
2 tablespoons freshly squeezed or store-bought orange juice
1 tablespoon white or red vinegar
1 tablespoon sugar

1. Preheat the oven to 450°F. Lightly oil the rack of a broiler pan or line a baking sheet with aluminum foil and oil the foil. Cut the tips off the chicken wings. Cut the wings into 2 pieces at the joint.

2. Toss the wing pieces with the salt and pepper. Set them on the prepared pan, leaving an inch or so between them. Roast until browned and fully cooked, about 30 minutes.

3. Meanwhile, stir the chipotle or adobo sauce, orange juice, vinegar, and sugar together in a small saucepan. Bring to a simmer over low heat and cook until syrupy and reduced by about half. Scrape into a medium mixing bowl.

4. Toss the cooked wings in the glaze and return them to the rack. There will be sauce left in the bowl; set it aside. Roast until the glaze starts to darken, about 5 minutes. Toss the wings in the bowl again and pile onto a serving plate. Let cool about 5 minutes before serving and pass plenty of napkins.

MAKES 16 PIECES

Hummus

Universally loved and easily thrown together, hummus makes an exotic side dish or appetizer with a minimal amount of work. Susan prefers it in a sandwich, with sliced cucumbers on pumpernickel bread.

One 15 ½-ounce can chickpeas, rinsed and drained
1 tablespoon fresh lemon juice
1 tablespoon toasted sesame oil
2 small garlic cloves, minced
¼ cup olive oil
¼ cup minced parsley
3 scallions, trimmed and thinly sliced
Salt and freshly ground black pepper

1. Combine the chickpeas, lemon juice, sesame oil, and garlic in the workbowl of a food processor fitted with the metal blade. Process until the chickpeas are finely chopped. Add the olive oil slowly with the motor running and continue processing until the hummus is the consistency of a coarse purée.

2. Transfer the hummus to a mixing bowl and stir in the parsley, scallions, and salt and pepper to taste. Store the hummus, covered, in the refrigerator up to 3 days. Bring to room temperature about ½ hour before serving.

MAKES 1 ¼ CUPS

Pita Chips

If the weather is not humid, you can make these up to a couple of days before you serve them. Store at room temperature in an airtight container.

Preheat the oven to 350°F. Split pita loaves into top and bottom rounds. Cut each round into 8 wedges. Brush a baking sheet (or two if making more chips than will fit on one baking sheet) lightly with olive or peanut oil. Toast the pita in the oven, turning and stirring twice, until lightly browned and crisp, about 10 minutes. Serve warm or cool.

Butternut Squash Soup

S̲our cream adds a sharp note to the rich sweetness of butternut squash purée.

Vegetable oil

1 small butternut squash (1 ¾ to 2 pounds)

2 tablespoons unsalted butter

1 large leek, cleaned (see page 5) and cut crosswise into ½-inch pieces

1 medium carrot, peeled, trimmed, and coarsely shredded

8 fresh sage leaves

½ teaspoon ground ginger

¼ teaspoon ground nutmeg

3 cups Chicken Broth (page 37) or store-bought chicken broth,
   or as needed

1 teaspoon salt, less if using canned broth

½ cup regular or reduced-fat sour cream

¼ cup very thinly sliced chives

1 tablespoon bourbon (optional)

1. Preheat the oven to 375°F. Line a baking sheet with aluminum foil and grease the foil lightly with oil.

2. Cut the squash in half crosswise. Stand the squash halves cut-side down on a cutting board and cut them again from top to bottom. Scoop out the seeds and the membrane that holds them in place. Set the squash, flesh-side down, on the prepared pan and bake until the flesh is tender when poked with a paring knife and the undersides are deep brown, about 1 hour. Remove and let stand until cool enough to handle.

3. Peel the skin off the squash pieces. Mash the flesh coarsely and set aside. Heat the butter in a heavy 4-quart saucepan over medium heat. Add the leek, carrot, and sage. Cook, stirring, until the leeks are wilted, about 4 minutes. Stir in the ginger and nutmeg, then pour in 3 cups of broth. Stir in the mashed squash and bring to a boil. Adjust the heat so the liquid is simmering. Season with salt, cover, and cook 10 minutes. Remove from the heat and cool to warm.

4. Put the sour cream, chives, and bourbon, if using, in a mixing bowl. Working in batches, blend the soup until smooth, adding additional broth if necessary to make a smooth but thick purée. Pour each batch into the mixing bowl. When all the soup is puréed, whisk everything together until no traces of sour cream remain. The soup can be prepared ahead to this point. Store, covered, in the refrigerator for up to 2 days.

5. Reheat the soup over medium-low heat, stirring often, just until simmering. Serve hot.

MAKES ABOUT 6 CUPS • SERVES 6 AS A FIRST COURSE

Lady Godiva

Lady Godiva was a woman so desperate to free her hometown of Coventry from the burden of heavy taxes placed on its residents by her husband, the Earl, that she agreed to ride naked on a horse through the market to convince him to abandon the tolls. In the story passed down through history, Godiva supposedly loosened her hair (in order to preserve her modesty) and made the journey on horseback surrounded by two knights.

Little is actually known about Lady Godiva, the wife of one of the most powerful men in England. Rumor and myth swirl around her story; even the date of her birth is unknown (sometime between A.D. 980 and A.D. 1000). It is difficult to form an accurate picture of her save for the fact that she was a powerful and wealthy woman during a time when this was quite unusual.

There is also much debate about Lady Godiva's lineage (was she born to royalty or did she marry into it?), her marriage (her husband is described as both a tyrant and a fair and merciful nobleman), and even her town of origin. Things changed so much that by the fourteenth century, the story shifted from one of female empowerment to a religious parable—namely, that a miracle took place that allowed a pious woman to ride through town in a state of undress and remain unobserved. The only thing that appears constant in all the stories is that our heroine was a woman of noble intent whose efforts had a great and genuine impact on the landscape at the time.

Ironically, it is likely that the most famous thing (in fact the only thing) Lady Godiva is known for *never* actually happened. Despite this, people still talk about her a thousand years later. Whether true or apocryphal, Lady Godiva's most desperate act seems to be burned into the public consciousness as well as the history books. Perhaps this is because the story of female empowerment—a mere 900 years before women's suffrage—is inspiring. Or maybe it's just that a naked woman riding bareback throughout town is salacious enough to keep people fascinated.

Foolproof Macaroni and Cheese

Salt

4 cups Béchamel Sauce (page 114)

1 pound small shells or elbow macaroni

½ pound coarsely shredded sharp Cheddar cheese (about 2 ½ cups)

½ pound coarsely shredded Gruyère or Emmenthaler cheese
  (about 2 ½ cups)

Freshly ground black pepper (optional)

½ cup coarse bread crumbs

¼ cup grated Parmesan cheese

2 tablespoons unsalted butter, melted

1. Bring a large pot of well-salted water to a boil. Make the Béchamel.

2. While the sauce is simmering, stir the macaroni into the boiling water and cook, stirring occasionally, until al dente—a layer of white should be clearly visible when you bite one piece in half—about 5 minutes. Drain immediately and rinse under cold water until the macaroni stops steaming. Shake the colander to get rid of as much water as possible. Transfer to a large mixing bowl.

3. Preheat the oven to 375°F.

4. When the sauce is done, remove from the heat and stir in the Cheddar and Gruyère or Emmenthaler. Taste and add salt and pepper if you like. Pour the sauce over the macaroni and stir until all the macaroni is coated evenly. Scrape the macaroni and cheese into an 11-inch oval baking dish or any casserole or baking dish that fits the macaroni comfortably.

5. Stir the bread crumbs, grated Parmesan, and melted butter together in a small bowl until the crumbs are evenly moistened with butter. Spread the crumb

CONTINUED

topping in an even layer over the top of the casserole. Bake the casserole immediately or keep at room temperature for up to 1 hour before baking. Bake until the top is well browned and the edges are bubbling, about 40 minutes. Let stand 5 minutes before serving.

SERVES 6 AS A MAIN COURSE
OR 10 AS A SIDE DISH

MIKE DELFINO, 39, is at the buffet table dishing up some food. He's good-looking in a blue-collar sort of way.

SUSAN walks by just in time to see Mike reach for the macaroni and cheese.

>SUSAN:
>
>Oh . . . I wouldn't eat that if I were you.

>MIKE:
>
>Why?

>SUSAN:
>
>I made it. Trust me.

Mike, completely charmed by Susan's candor, starts to scoop a big mouthful of the macaroni and cheese. Susan stops him.

>SUSAN:
>
>Hey! Hey, do you have a death wish?

>MIKE:
>
>No, I just refuse to believe that anyone could screw up macaroni and cheese.

Mike EATS the mac 'n cheese. He instantly grimaces.

>MIKE:
>
>Omigod! How did you . . . ? It tastes like it's burned and undercooked.

>SUSAN:
>
>Yeah. I get that a lot. Here you go.

SUSAN hands him a napkin. After he discreetly spits out the food, they both start laughing.

Vegetarian Chili

Bottles labeled "chili powder" contain a mix of ingredients, including (usually) some type of ground dried chili pepper, cumin, oregano, salt, and a host of unpronounceable additives. If you have a favorite one of these, feel free to use it to taste in place of the salt, cumin, ground chili, and oregano listed below. But by creating your own chili powder, you have more control over the individual elements. (For single-chili powders, see Sources, page 266.)

3 tablespoons vegetable oil

2 medium yellow onions, cut into ½-inch dice (about 2 cups)

1 large red bell pepper, cored, seeded, and cut into ¼-inch dice (about 1 ½ cups)

2 medium carrots, peeled, trimmed, and cut into ¼-inch dice (about 1 cup)

6 garlic cloves, minced

1 pound large mushrooms, stems trimmed, caps cut in half and then into ¼-inch slices (about 6 cups)

1 teaspoon salt

2 teaspoons ground single-chili powder (see Note)

1 ½ teaspoons ground coriander seed

1 teaspoon ground cumin

1 teaspoon dried oregano

Two 14 ½-ounce cans diced tomatoes with liquid

Two 15-ounce cans kidney beans, drained and rinsed

½ cup finely chopped fresh cilantro

1 cup sour cream (optional)

1 medium red onion, finely chopped (optional)

1. Heat the oil in a heavy 4- to 5-quart saucepan over medium heat until rippling. Add the onions, bell pepper, carrots, and garlic, and cook, stirring, until the onion is lightly browned, about 8 minutes.

2. Stir in the mushrooms, sprinkle the salt over the vegetables, and continue cooking until the liquid given up by the mushrooms is cooked off. Add the chili powder, coriander, cumin, and oregano, and cook until fragrant. Pour in the

CONTINUED

tomatoes and their liquid and bring to a boil. Adjust the heat so the liquid is simmering. Cover and cook until the vegetables are very tender, about 10 minutes.

3. Stir in the beans and cook until heated through. Stir in the cilantro. Serve hot in bowls, passing the sour cream and chopped red onion separately, if using.

MAKES 3 QUARTS • SERVES 6 AS A MAIN COURSE

Note: It has become easier to find all types of single-chili powders, not only in specialty stores, but in the spice aisles of supermarkets as well. Here, in order of increasing heat, are some you may find: ancho, pasilla, de arbol, and pequin. Chipotle powder is made by grinding smoked dried jalapeño chilies; it packs quite a bit of heat plus a mysterious, smoky flavor. If you see some, pick it up; it is a fine addition to any pot of chili.

Sophie's Meatballs

This is the one recipe passed down from Susan's mother that's worth spending the time preparing in the kitchen. In fact, Susan can remember being a little girl and watching her mother in the kitchen carefully shaping the meatballs into perfectly round balls. For some reason, it's also the one dish that Susan is actually able to pull off every other time she makes it. In fact, it's so good that Julie even asked Susan if she can teach her how to make the recipe.

1 tablespoon olive oil

1 small onion, very finely chopped (about ½ cup)

1 egg

2 tablespoons chopped fresh parsley

Large pinch of nutmeg, preferably freshly grated

1 pound ground beef or ½ pound each ground beef and ground pork

¼ cup grated Parmesan cheese

¼ cup bread crumbs

Vegetable oil cooking spray

1. Heat the olive oil in a small skillet over medium heat. Stir in the onion and cook, stirring occasionally, until the onion just begins to brown, about 8 minutes. Remove from the heat and scrape into a medium bowl. Let stand until warm.

2. Add the egg, parsley, and nutmeg to the onion. Beat with a fork until thoroughly blended. Crumble the beef (and pork, if using) into the bowl. Sprinkle the cheese and bread crumbs over the meat. Mix together thoroughly with your hands or a wooden spoon until the parsley is evenly distributed. Cover and refrigerate 15 minutes. (Chilling will make it easier to form meatballs.)

3. Place an oven rack about 6 inches from the broiler and preheat the broiler to the highest setting. Spray the rack of a broiler pan with vegetable oil cooking spray. Using ¼ cup mix for each, form 2-inch meatballs, placing them on the prepared rack as you go.

CONTINUED

4. Broil the meatballs until well browned on top, about 6 minutes. The underside should be browned as well. If not, flip the meatballs and broil 1 to 2 minutes until the top side is browned.

5. Eat as is (check for doneness and if necessary bake in a 350°F oven until no trace of pink remains at the center), or add to Light Tomato Sauce (see opposite page) or the tomato sauce of your choice and simmer for 20 minutes.

VARIATION

Chicken Meatballs

Substitute an equal amount of ground chicken (preferably ground chicken thighs) for the beef and/or pork. Add an additional 2 tablespoons bread crumbs and beat 1 tablespoon of olive oil together with the eggs and parsley.

Pasta with Light Tomato Sauce
(with or without Sophie's Meatballs)

The key to this light, fresh-tasting sauce is to start with packaged strained tomatoes—not the much thicker canned tomato purée or crushed tomatoes. (See the Note on page 98 for alternatives.)

FOR THE LIGHT TOMATO SAUCE

3 tablespoons olive oil

2 medium yellow onions, cut into ¼-inch dice (about 2 cups)

4 garlic cloves, minced

1 teaspoon dried oregano

½ teaspoon crushed hot red pepper

Two 28-ounce sterile-pack containers strained tomatoes,
    such as Pomì

2 bay leaves

1 ½ teaspoons kosher salt, plus more for cooking the pasta

FOR THE PASTA

1 pound ziti, rigatoni, or penne pasta

¼ cup chopped fresh basil or Italian parsley

Sophie's Meatballs (page 95), optional

Grated Parmesan cheese

1. Bring a large pot of salted water to a boil.

2. Heat the olive oil in a heavy 3- to 4-quart nonaluminum pot over medium heat. Add the onions and cook, stirring occasionally, until they turn clear, about 6 minutes. Stir in the garlic, oregano, and red pepper. Cook 2 minutes.

3. Stir in the tomatoes, bay leaves, and 1 ½ teaspoons salt. Raise the heat to high and bring the sauce to a boil, stirring. Adjust the heat so the sauce is at a lively simmer. Cook, stirring occasionally, 20 minutes.

CONTINUED

TO SERVE THE SAUCE WITHOUT MEATBALLS:

After the sauce has been simmering 10 minutes, stir the pasta into the water. Stir gently until the water returns to a boil. Cook, stirring occasionally, until the pasta is al dente, about 9 minutes. Drain the pasta and return to the pot off the heat. Stir the basil or parsley into the sauce. Ladle enough of the sauce into the pot over low heat to coat the pasta evenly. Remove from the heat and stir in a handful of grated Parmesan. Ladle into warm bowls or a warm platter. Serve, passing additional grated cheese and sauce, if desired.

TO SERVE THE SAUCE WITH MEATBALLS:

Prepare and broil the meatballs while the sauce is simmering. After the sauce has simmered 20 minutes, slip the meatballs into the sauce. Cook 20 minutes.

After the meatballs have been cooking 10 minutes, cook and sauce the pasta as described above, stirring the basil or parsley into the sauce just before ladling over the pasta. Serve meatballs along with each serving of pasta or arrange in the center of the platter.

In either case, refrigerate the remaining sauce for up to 3 days or freeze up to 1 month.

MAKES 7 CUPS (ENOUGH TO SAUCE 1 POUND OF PASTA
AND FREEZE AN EQUAL AMOUNT)

Note: If sterile-pack strained tomatoes are not available, substitute two 35-ounce cans of whole plum tomatoes and pass them through a food mill fitted with a fine disc.

Baked Stuffed Shells

Think of these as self-contained lasagnas, each pasta shell filled with a mix of cheeses and spinach. Stuffed shells are good for buffets and larger gatherings, but even if yours is a smaller group, make the full recipe. They freeze beautifully.

Light Tomato Sauce (page 97)
Salt
1 pound jumbo pasta shells (45 to 50)
One 10-ounce package frozen chopped spinach, defrosted
3 cups whole milk or part-skim ricotta cheese
½ pound packaged or fresh mozzarella cheese, grated (about 2 cups)
2 ounces ham, cut into ¼-inch dice (½ cup), optional
⅓ cup grated Parmesan cheese, plus more for the top of the casserole
1 egg

1. Make the sauce and simmer 20 minutes.

2. While it is simmering, bring a large pot of salted water to a boil. Stir in the shells and cook, stirring gently occasionally, until tender but still quite firm, about 9 minutes. Drain and rinse them under cold water, handling them gently to keep them from breaking apart.

3. Squeeze as much of the water from the spinach as possible. Beat the spinach, ricotta cheese, mozzarella, ham, if using, ⅓ cup Parmesan, and egg together in a mixing bowl until well blended.

4. Place a rack in the center position and preheat the oven to 350°F. Ladle about 1 cup sauce into each of two 11 x 13-inch baking dishes to coat the bottoms. Using about 1 slightly rounded tablespoonful of filling for each, fill the shells completely but do not overstuff. Line the filled shells side by side in the baking dishes.

5. Spoon an even layer of tomato sauce over the tops of the shells and cover the dishes tightly with aluminum foil. (The shells can be prepared to this point and

CONTINUED

refrigerated for up to 3 days or frozen for up to 6 weeks. Defrost frozen shells in the refrigerator overnight before baking.) Bake 30 minutes (40 minutes for refrigerated shells).

6. Uncover, sprinkle grated Parmesan cheese liberally over the tops of the casseroles, and continue baking until the cheese is lightly browned and the sauce is bubbling, about 15 minutes. Let stand 10 minutes before serving. Heat and pass any remaining sauce separately.

SERVES 8 (IN TWO BAKING DISHES,
MAKING IT EASY TO FREEZE HALF)

Newfangled Noodle Casserole

With the exception of the chicken, the ingredients for this updated casserole can be kept on hand. Because the noodles aren't cooked first, the casserole can be in the oven 10 minutes after you come home from work. Forty effortless minutes later, it is ready.

One 1-quart container chicken broth

One 10 ¾-ounce can condensed cream of mushroom soup

1 pound boneless, skinless chicken thighs or breasts, cut into 1-inch pieces

3 cups frozen broccoli "cuts" (not whole stalks)

3 cups wide curly egg noodles

1 cup coarsely shredded Swiss or Gruyère cheese

OPTIONAL TOPPING

¼ cup homemade coarse bread crumbs (page 213), panko, or plain packaged bread crumbs

¼ cup grated Parmesan cheese

1 tablespoon butter, melted

1. Preheat the oven to 400°F.

2. Whisk the chicken broth and soup together in a medium saucepan. Heat over medium heat to simmering. Meanwhile, stir the chicken and broccoli together in an 11 x 13-inch baking dish. Add the noodles and Swiss or Gruyère cheese and stir again until all the ingredients are evenly distributed. Pour the soup mixture into the baking dish, wiggle the dish to distribute the sauce, and cover tightly with aluminum foil. Bake 30 minutes.

3. Meanwhile, if using the optional topping, stir the crumbs, Parmesan cheese, and melted butter together until the crumbs are evenly moistened.

4. Uncover the casserole and sprinkle the topping, if using, over it. Continue baking until the top or topping is golden brown and the liquid is thickened, about 10 minutes. Let stand 5 minutes before serving.

SERVES 6

Chicken and Dumplings

One 4-pound chicken, cut into eighths

4 medium carrots, peeled and cut crosswise into ½-inch rounds

2 celery stalks, trimmed and cut on the bias into ½-inch slices

2 cups frozen pearl onions or 1 medium yellow onion,
cut into ½-inch strips

4 cups Chicken Broth (page 37) or one 1-quart container
store-bought chicken broth

½ teaspoon dried thyme

Salt and freshly ground black pepper

1 ½ cups all-purpose flour

1 tablespoon finely chopped fresh parsley (optional)

2 ¼ teaspoons baking powder

1 teaspoon salt

3 tablespoons unsalted butter

¾ cup milk

1. Trim any overhanging fat from the chicken pieces. Cut the chicken breasts in half crosswise, using a heavy, sharp knife. Put the chicken pieces and any giblets (minus the liver) in a Dutch oven or flameproof casserole into which they fit in a single layer (an 11-inch-wide by 5-inch-deep pot works well). Scatter the carrots, celery, and pearl onions over them and add the broth. Pour in enough water to cover the chicken and vegetables by 1 inch. Add the thyme and season lightly with salt and pepper. Bring to a boil over high heat. Boil for 2 minutes, skimming the foam and fat from the surface. Adjust the heat so the liquid is simmering and cover the pot. Cook until no trace of pink remains near the bone of the thigh pieces, about 50 minutes.

2. About 10 minutes before the chicken is fully cooked, make the dumplings: Stir the flour, parsley, if using, baking powder, and 1 teaspoon salt together in a medium mixing bowl. Work the butter into the flour with your fingertips until

the butter resembles miniature cornflakes and is distributed evenly through the flour. Pour the milk into the bowl and stir gently just until the flour is moistened. Don't overmix. A few lumps and a streak or two of flour are fine.

3. Fish out the back, neck, and giblets (if there) from the pot and discard them. Make sure there is enough liquid to barely cover the chicken and vegetables. (If there is more, ladle some off and reserve it for another use; if there is less, pour in broth or water and let the pot liquid return to a boil before continuing.) Adjust the heat so the liquid is at a steady simmer. Drop the dumpling batter by heaping tablespoonfuls onto the liquid, leaving at least 1½ inches between them. Cover the pot and cook until the dumplings are light and fluffy and cooked through, about 12 minutes.

4. To serve: Use a slotted spoon to transfer the dumplings into shallow serving bowls. Add two pieces of chicken and some vegetables to each bowl. Ladle some of the liquid over the chicken, serving as much of the liquid as you like.

SERVES 4

Note: Once the chicken is cooked, the dish can sit off the heat for an hour or so before you add the dumplings. The dumplings, however, should be cooked as soon as the batter is made and the whole served as soon as the dumplings are cooked.

Asian-y Turkey Burgers

1 ½ pounds ground turkey
2 tablespoons soy sauce
2 scallions, trimmed and finely chopped
Freshly ground black pepper
Oil for cooking

1. Crumble the turkey into a mixing bowl. Drizzle the soy sauce over the turkey and add the scallions and several generous grindings of pepper. Mix the seasoning through the turkey until evenly distributed. Divide the turkey into 4 equal portions and form each into a 1-inch-thick patty. Chill at least 1 hour or up to overnight.

2. To panfry: Heat a griddle or heavy pan large enough to hold the burgers over medium heat. Lightly grease the pan with oil and cook the burgers, turning once, until well browned and no trace of pink remains at the center, about 12 minutes. (An instant-reading thermometer inserted into the thickest part of the burger will register 165°F.) The burgers may also be grilled. Grease the grill with a paper towel dipped in oil before setting the burgers on it.

MAKES 4 BURGERS

Shopping Bag Chicken

Even Susan would have a difficult time ruining this one (although one suspects she would pull off a minor miracle and find a way). Next time you're at the market, be sure to ask the bagger for paper, not plastic, since this recipe, as the name would indicate, includes a paper bag as a necessary ingredient.

4 medium new potatoes, scrubbed and cut into quarters (about ¾ pound)

1 tablespoon olive oil

1 teaspoon salt, plus more for seasoning the vegetables

¼ teaspoon freshly ground black pepper, plus more
    for seasoning the vegetables

3 links sweet or hot Italian sausage (about ¾ pound),
    cut into 1 ½-inch lengths (optional)

1 teaspoon dried thyme

½ teaspoon oregano

½ teaspoon paprika

One 4-pound chicken, cut into eighths

3 small zucchini (about 5 ounces each), trimmed and
    cut into ½-inch rounds

1. Set a rack in the center position and preheat the oven to 425°F. Toss the potatoes together with the olive oil in a large (about 18 x 13-inch) roasting pan. Season with salt and pepper and toss again. Mix in the sausage pieces, if using, and scrape the potatoes and sausage toward the center of the pan.

2. Put the thyme, oregano, paprika, 1 teaspoon salt, and ¼ teaspoon pepper into a brown paper bag. Stir the spices and spread them out in a more or less even layer over the bottom of the bag. Trim any excess fat from the chicken pieces and pat them dry with paper towels. Add them to the bag, crimp the top to seal it tightly, and shake the bag to coat the chicken evenly with the spices. Arrange the seasoned chicken pieces, skin-side up, around the edges of the pan. Roast 15 minutes.

CONTINUED

3. Add the zucchini to the center of the pan and stir to mix with the sausage and potatoes. Be as fussy (or not) as you like now and the next time you stir the vegetables: Turn them one by one to brown each piece evenly or just give them a big stir. Roast 15 minutes.

4. Stir (or turn) the vegetables and sausage one more time, keeping them in the center of the pan. Roast until no trace of pink remains at the thickest part of the chicken thighs, about 20 minutes.

5. Remove the chicken to a serving platter and scatter the vegetables and sausages around it. Depending on the chicken and sausage, you may want to make a brief pit stop on a paper towel–lined baking sheet to drain the meats and vegetables before putting them on the platter.

SERVES 4 GENEROUSLY,

6 IF PREPARED WITH SAUSAGE

Basic Crepes

B ree has tried several times to show Susan how to make this basic food. Unfortunately, Susan has never been able to master it. In fact, Bree will disavow any knowledge of ever giving Susan this recipe. (If you've tasted Susan's abomination of a crepe, you would understand.)

For most people, however, crepes are easily mastered. The batter or the crepes themselves can be refrigerated for several days. Once made, they can be filled with everything from spinach and ham (see page 111) to peanut butter and jelly.

1 cup milk, at room temperature

2 large eggs

2 tablespoons unsalted butter, melted, plus more for cooking the crepes

1 teaspoon sugar

¼ teaspoon salt

¾ cup plus 2 tablespoons all-purpose flour

1. Put the milk, eggs, 2 tablespoons melted butter, sugar, and salt in a blender. Blend until smooth. Add the flour and blend, using short bursts, just until the batter is smooth. Pour the batter into a container, cover, and refrigerate at least 4 hours or up to overnight.

2. Heat a 6- or 8-inch crepe pan (measured across the inside bottom) or a heavy nonstick pan over medium-low heat until a few drops of water flicked into the pan dance for 2 to 3 seconds before evaporating. Any shorter, lower the heat; any longer, raise it a little. Brush the pan with melted butter or use a folded paper towel dipped in the melted butter. Pour the required amount of batter— 1½ tablespoons for a 6-inch crepe or 3 tablespoons for an 8-inch crepe—into the center of the pan. Working quickly, tilt and wiggle the pan so the batter coats the bottom of the pan in an even layer. (See the box on page 110 for more crepe-making pointers.) Return the pan to the heat and cook until the underside is a lacy golden brown, about 1½ minutes. Turn and cook until the spots on the underside are golden brown, about 2 minutes. (The two sides of a crepe will have distinctly different appearances; when filling or serving, make sure to

CONTINUED

present them lacy, not spotty, side out.) Remove to a plate, repeating with the remaining batter and stacking the crepes on the plate. Butter the pan every second or third crepe. Finished crepes can be held at room temperature for up to 6 hours or refrigerated for up to 3 days. Bring refrigerated crepes to room temperature before serving them.

MAKES 1 ¾ CUPS BATTER, ENOUGH FOR
ABOUT TWENTY 6-INCH OR TEN 8-INCH CREPES

About Crepes

- If this is the first time you are making crepes, go ahead and make a double batch of batter. It will take several crepes in order to get the hang of things. No worries, though; unused batter can be stored in the refrigerator for up to 3 days.

- French chefs will tell you that a crepe pan—made of blue steel with short sloping sides and a perfectly flat bottom—is the best way to make crepes. And they may be right. But French crepe pans are also costly and somewhat tricky to season and maintain. A good, heavy nonstick pan will perform beautifully. Just remember to measure the pan across the inside bottom to get an accurate idea of how large your crepes will be.

- The idea is to get the right amount of batter into the pan as quickly as possible and then, also as quickly as possible, spread the batter into an even layer before the batter starts to cook. The best way to do this is to find a measure that holds the right amount of batter—1 ½ or 3 tablespoons—for the crepe size being made. A coffee measure, tiny ladle, or gravy spoon may do the trick.

- Especially when you first start out, don't worry if the crepes are irregularly formed. You will soon have the knack of making beautiful, lacy, round crepes.

Filled Crepes

Crepes are like pasta; they pair well with any number of ingredients. For a simple dessert or snack, spread half a crepe lightly with jam or jelly. Fold the uncovered half over the filling, then fold again into a triangle. Warm the crepes on a baking sheet in a 200°F oven before sprinkling with powdered sugar. (Nutella chocolate-hazelnut spread is delicious as a filling, too.)

Spinach-Ham Filling

1 ½ pounds fresh spinach
2 tablespoons unsalted butter
4 scallions, trimmed and thinly sliced
1 ¼ cups ricotta cheese
4 ounces smoked ham, cut into ¼-inch dice (about 1 cup)
¼ cup grated Parmesan cheese
Salt and freshly ground black pepper

1. Remove the stems from the spinach. Wash in plenty of cool water to remove all sand and grit. Spin as dry as possible in a salad spinner. Stack several leaves at a time and cut them crosswise into roughly ½-inch strips

2. Heat the butter in a large (about 12-inch) pan over medium heat until bubbling. Add the scallions and cook, stirring, until wilted, about 2 minutes. Stir in half the spinach and cook until it starts to wilt. Add the remaining spinach, a handful at a time, as room becomes available in the pan. Cook just until all the spinach is bright green and wilted. Scrape into a bowl and cool.

3. Stir in the ricotta, ham, and Parmesan. Season with salt, if necessary, and pepper. The filling can be made up to a day before using. Cover and refrigerate until needed.

MAKES 4 CUPS FILLING,
ENOUGH FOR EIGHT 8-INCH CREPES

Chicken-Mushroom Filling

2 tablespoons olive oil

1 pound large mushrooms, stem ends trimmed, caps cut in half,
    then into ¼-inch slices (about 6 cups)

Salt

2 cups coarsely shredded or chopped cooked chicken

1 cup coarsely grated Swiss cheese

1 cup Béchamel Sauce (page 114)

Freshly ground black pepper

1. Heat the oil in a large (about 12-inch) skillet over medium heat. Add the mushrooms and season lightly with salt. Cook, stirring, until the mushrooms release their liquid, the liquid is evaporated, and the mushrooms start to brown, about 8 minutes. Scrape into a bowl and cool.

2. Stir in the chicken, cheese, and béchamel. Season to taste with salt and pepper. The filling can be made up to a day before using. Cover and refrigerate until needed.

MAKES 4 CUPS FILLING,
ENOUGH FOR EIGHT 8-INCH CREPES

Baking Stuffed Crepes

Eight 8-inch Basic Crepes (page 109)
Spinach-Ham Filling (page 111) or Chicken-Mushroom Filling
    (opposite page)
Melted butter

OPTIONAL TOPPINGS

1 cup coarsely grated Swiss cheese
¼ cup grated Parmesan cheese
1 cup Béchamel Sauce (page 114)

Heat the oven to 350°F. Spread a scant ½ cup of filling over the bottom third of a crepe, leaving a 1-inch border uncovered. Fold the bottom of the crepe, then the sides, over the filling; then roll into a compact tube shape. Place, seam-side down, in a buttered 8 x 11-inch baking dish. The simplest way to serve the crepes is to bake them as is until the filling is warmed through and the tops of the crepes are crispy in spots, about 25 minutes. If desired, sprinkle both cheeses over the top before baking. Or, for a richer version, spread the tops of the filled crepes with the béchamel, then top with both cheeses. Bake crepes topped with béchamel and cheese until the sauce and cheese are well browned and the edges are bubbling, about 35 minutes.

SERVES 4

Béchamel Sauce

4 tablespoons unsalted butter
¼ cup all-purpose flour
1 quart hot milk
1 ½ teaspoons salt
¼ teaspoon freshly ground black pepper
Large pinch of nutmeg, preferably freshly grated

1. Heat the butter in a heavy 3-quart saucepan over medium-low heat until foaming. Whisk in the flour. Continue cooking, whisking constantly, 4 minutes.

2. Pour the hot milk slowly into the flour mixture, whisking constantly. Pay special attention to the corners; that is where the sauce will stick and burn first. When all the milk is added, whisk constantly until the sauce comes to a boil. Adjust the heat so the sauce is simmering. Cook and simmer until lightly thickened, about 5 minutes. Season to taste with salt, pepper, and nutmeg. Use the sauce immediately, or scrape into a bowl and cover with a piece of plastic wrap pressed directly to the surface and store at room temperature for up to 2 hours. Refrigerating the sauce will affect its texture.

MAKES 4 CUPS

SUSAN'S
SHOPPING LIST

Band-Aids
gauze bandages
Hydrogen peroxide
cotton swabs
Healthy Choice frozen
meals

Organic

apples

bananas

pears

navel oranges

blueberry bars

apple bars

granola

cereal

lettuce

oatmeal

milk

Dr. Phil book

Merlot

Chardonnay

Diet Coke

Breyers nonfat ice cream

Kraft Macaroni & Cheese

Oprah magazine

frozen pizza

baked Lay's chips

Hot & Spicy Cheez-Its

anti-anxiety medicine

Sloppy Joes, Two Ways

By definition, this is a messy meal. Susan's version includes a few more and unusual ingredients to give it an extra kick. While one might normally be leery of Susan being inventive when it comes to food, this is the rare case when the dish actually turns out tastier than the classic version.

USE REGULAR
PAPRIKA FOR A
MILDER VERSION;
HOT OR SMOKED
PAPRIKA (BOTH
ARE IMPORTED
FROM SPAIN AND
HUNGARY) FOR
MORE OF A KICK.
SEE SOURCES,
PAGE 266.

1 tablespoon vegetable oil

1 large yellow onion, diced (about 2 cups)

1 large celery stalk, trimmed and diced (about ½ cup)

Salt

1 pound ground beef or turkey

1 teaspoon paprika

1 ½ cups canned diced tomatoes, with liquid

3 tablespoons Worcestershire sauce

Hot red pepper sauce to taste

4 large soft rolls or 2 cups uncooked elbow or small shell macaroni

Grated Cheddar cheese (optional)

1. Heat the oil in a large heavy skillet over medium heat. Add the onion and celery and season lightly with salt. Cook, stirring, until wilted, about 4 minutes. Crumble the ground beef or turkey into the pan and cook, stirring and mashing to break up clumps, until it loses its pink color and the liquid given off is evaporated, about 4 minutes.

2. Add the paprika, cook for a minute, then pour in the tomatoes and their liquid. Bring to a boil, stir in the Worcestershire sauce, and adjust the heat so the liquid is at a slow bowl. Cook, stirring often, until there is just enough liquid to lightly coat the turkey and vegetables, about 15 minutes. Stir in hot red pepper sauce and salt to taste. Serve hot or cool and store, covered, in the refrigerator for up to 3 days.

TO SERVE AS SANDWICHES:

Lightly toast the rolls under the broiler if you like. Spoon about 1 cup of the sloppy Joes over the bottom of the roll and sprinkle grated Cheddar over it if you like before topping with the other half of the roll.

TO SERVE WITH MACARONI:

Cook the macaroni in a large pot of salted water until tender but not mushy. Reserve about ½ cup of the cooking liquid and drain the macaroni. Return the macaroni to the pot, scrape in the sloppy Joe mixture, and stir to mix. Check the seasoning and add as much of the reserved cooking liquid as necessary to help the sauce glide over the macaroni. Serve in warm bowls, topped with grated Cheddar if you like.

MAKES 4 CUPS, ENOUGH FOR 4 SANDWICHES
OR 6 SERVINGS WHEN MIXED WITH MACARONI

Side Dishes

Garlic Mashed Potatoes

There are two schools of thought when it comes to mashed potatoes. Half the people like their potatoes smooth and silky. Susan likes hers a little lumpy. Use a handheld electric mixer for the former, a potato masher for the latter.

2 large baking (Idaho) potatoes (about 1 ½ pounds)
Salt
10 garlic cloves, sliced
½ cup milk or light cream
4 tablespoons unsalted butter, cut into little pieces
Freshly ground black pepper

1. Peel the potatoes and wash them. Cut them into 2-inch chunks, dropping the pieces into a 2-quart saucepan of water as you go. Toss in a small handful of salt and the garlic. Bring to a boil. Cook until the potatoes are tender when poked with a small knife but still intact, about 15 minutes. Don't overcook.

2. Drain the potatoes and garlic and return them to the pan. Let stand, uncovered, 2 to 3 minutes. Add the milk and butter to the pan and set over low heat until the butter is melted. Beat everything in the pan together with a wire whisk, potato masher, or handheld mixer until the potatoes are as smooth or lumpy as you like. Season to taste with salt and pepper and serve hot.

SERVES 4

Easy or Easier Coleslaw

If you choose the Easy option, use a small head of green cabbage or the rest of the head of Savoy cabbage from Stuffed Cabbage (page 44).

FOR THE DRESSING

> ½ cup mayonnaise
> 2 tablespoons white vinegar
> 1 tablespoon sugar
> ¾ teaspoon salt
> ½ teaspoon celery seed

FOR THE EASY SLAW

> 1 small green cabbage (about 1 ½ pounds)
> 2 medium carrots, peeled and trimmed

FOR THE EASIER SLAW

> One 1-pound bag coleslaw mix

1. Make the dressing: Whisk the mayonnaise, vinegar, sugar, salt, and celery seed in a small bowl.

2. For the Easy Slaw: Cut the cabbage through the core into wedges small enough to fit through the food tube of the food processor. Cut out the core from each wedge. Set up the food processor with the thinnest slicing disc in place. Slice all the cabbage, removing it as necessary to a 1-gallon sealable plastic bag. Switch to the coarse grating blade and shred all the carrots. Add to the cabbage. (Alternately, cut the cabbage and grate the carrots by hand.) For the Easier Slaw: Simply transfer the coleslaw mix to a 1-gallon sealable bag.

3. Scrape all of the dressing into the bag. Remove most of the air from the bag (leave a little in, though) and seal the bag. Massage the contents of the bag to coat the vegetables with the dressing. Refrigerate, massaging occasionally, at least 4 hours or up to 2 days, until the cabbage is wilted and the dressing coats the slaw generously. Check for salt and serve. The coleslaw can be stored up to 4 days.

MAKES 3 CUPS

Spicy Slaw

Substitute the liquid from a jar of spicy peppers—peperoncini or cherry peppers, for example—for the vinegar.

Barbecued Slaw

Stir 2 tablespoons of your favorite barbecue sauce into the finished slaw.

Skillet Asparagus, with Variations

1 pound medium asparagus (stalks about ½-inch thick)
1 tablespoon butter, thinly sliced
Salt and freshly ground black pepper

1. Prep the asparagus: Hold the tip of each stalk in one hand and bend the end of the stalk with the other. The tough ends of the stalks will snap off; discard them. (The stalks may vary in length after snapping.) Peel the asparagus with a vegetable peeler from the end of the stalk to about an inch from the tip.

2. Put 2 tablespoons water in a 10-inch skillet. Lay the asparagus in the skillet and scatter the butter slices over them. Heat over medium-low heat until the water is simmering. Season the asparagus lightly with salt and pepper. Cover and cook until the thickest part of the stalks is tender but firm, about 4 minutes. Uncover, raise the heat to high, and cook until the water is evaporated and the asparagus begins to sizzle. Transfer the asparagus to a serving plate and serve hot.

VARIATIONS

Skillet Asparagus with Orange

Add the grated zest of 1 orange to the pan along with the water and butter.

Skillet Asparagus with Nuts

After the liquid is evaporated from the pan, scatter 3 tablespoons toasted and chopped hazelnuts, almonds, or pine nuts over the asparagus.

SERVES 4

Slow-Roasted String Beans

Here is another Susan-proof recipe. Toss string beans together with sliced garlic, olive oil, and salt and let them do their thing in a moderately hot oven. Stir once or twice as they cook and you're good to go.

1 pound string beans, ends trimmed
2 tablespoons olive oil
8 garlic cloves, not so thinly sliced
Salt
2 or 3 lemon wedges (optional)

1. Preheat the oven to 375°F.

2. Toss the string beans in an 11 x 13-inch baking dish with the oil, garlic, and a sprinkling of salt. Bake, stirring well 2 or 3 times, until very tender and browned in spots, about 40 minutes. Serve hot or at room temperature, with lemon if desired.

SERVES 4

Shortcut Polenta

Traditionally, making polenta takes a good 45 minutes of constant stirring. "Instant" polenta is a harried cook's good friend—a comforting side dish on the plate in less time than it takes to boil a potato or mix a box of macaroni and cheese.

1 cup "instant" polenta
1 ½ teaspoons salt
2 tablespoons unsalted butter or olive oil
¼ cup grated Parmesan cheese (optional)

1. Stir the polenta, 3 ½ cups water, and the salt together in a 2-quart saucepan. Place over medium heat and cook, stirring, until the water comes to a boil. Adjust the heat so the water is simmering and cook, stirring, until the polenta reaches the texture of very thick mashed potatoes, about 4 minutes. Add more water, if necessary, to get the right texture.

2. Remove from the heat and whisk in the butter or oil and cheese, if using. Serve immediately. At most, the polenta can be kept hot, tightly covered and off the heat, for 5 minutes. After that, it will start to firm up.

SERVES 4

◄◄ IF A BOX OF POLENTA ISN'T LABELED "INSTANT," IT STILL MAY BE. CHECK THE COOKING DIRECTIONS; IF THE SUGGESTED COOKING TIME IS 5 MINUTES OR LESS, YOU'VE GOT INSTANT POLENTA. IF IT IS MORE IN THE 30-MINUTE RANGE, IT IS THE TRADITIONAL, SLOW-COOKING TYPE. SEE SOURCES, PAGE 266.

VARIATION

Pour the finished polenta into a lightly oiled 8-inch round cake pan. Let stand until cooled and firm. (The polenta may be made up to 3 days in advance and refrigerated.) Set a rack in the center position and preheat the oven to 450°F. Cut the polenta into 8 wedges. Brush all sides of each wedge generously with olive oil and place on a baking sheet. Bake until light golden brown and crisp, about 20 minutes.

Fudge Cake or Cupcakes

2 cups all-purpose flour, plus more for the pans

½ cup unsweetened cocoa

1 ½ teaspoons baking powder

½ teaspoon salt

1 ½ sticks (12 tablespoons) unsalted butter, at room temperature,
   plus more for the pans

1 ½ cups sugar

3 large eggs, at room temperature

2 teaspoons pure vanilla extract

1 cup plus 2 tablespoons milk, at room temperature

1. Place a rack in the center position and preheat the oven to 350°F. Flour and butter two 9-inch round cake pans. (See Note on page 245 for baking cupcakes from this batter.)

2. Stir the flour, cocoa, baking powder, and salt together in a bowl. Set aside. Beat the butter and sugar in the bowl of an electric mixer (or in a large mixing bowl using a handheld mixer) at high speed until light and fluffy, a full 4 to 5 minutes. Add the eggs one at a time, beating very well after each, then beat in the vanilla. Add half the dry ingredients and mix at low speed until incorporated. Pour in the milk and mix at low speed until almost completely incorporated, then add the remaining dry ingredients. Beat at low speed just until the dry ingredients are incorporated and the batter looks smooth.

3. Divide the batter between the prepared pans. Bake until the cakes pull away from the sides of the pan and the center of the cake springs back when lightly pressed in the center, about 30 minutes. Cool in the pans 30 minutes before removing. Cool completely on the rack before serving or frosting.

MAKES TWO 9-INCH LAYERS OR 20 CUPCAKES

Caramel Frosting

This is a cream-based icing, so once the cake is frosted, it should be refrigerated immediately. Remove it to room temperature about 30 minutes before serving to take the chill off both the cake and the icing.

2 cups heavy cream
10 ounces small soft caramels (about 50 pieces), unwrapped

1. In a large saucepan, heat the cream and caramels over very low heat, whisking occasionally, until the caramels are completely dissolved. Scrape the mixture into a bowl and cover with a piece of plastic wrap applied directly to the surface. Refrigerate until thoroughly chilled.

2. Beat the caramel cream with a handheld mixer at high speed until light, fluffy, and a smooth spreading consistency. The frosting can be prepared up to a day in advance. Cover and refrigerate until needed.

MAKES 3 ½ CUPS, ENOUGH TO FILL
AND FROST A TWO-LAYER CAKE OR ICE 16 CUPCAKES

Chocolate-Butterscotch Bars

Vegetable oil cooking spray
3 cups all-purpose flour
1 ½ teaspoons baking powder
¾ teaspoon salt
2 sticks (16 tablespoons) unsalted butter, at room temperature
1 cup granulated sugar
1 cup packed light brown sugar
3 large eggs
2 teaspoons pure vanilla extract
1 cup chocolate chips
1 cup butterscotch chips

1. Set a rack in the center position and preheat the oven to 350°F. Grease a 13 x 9-inch cake pan with cooking spray.

2. Stir the flour, baking powder, and salt together in a small bowl. Set aside. Beat the butter and sugars together in the bowl of an electric mixer (or in a mixing bowl using a handheld mixer) at high speed until very light and fluffy, about 4 minutes. Add the eggs one at a time and beat well after each. Beat in the vanilla extract.

3. Switch to a rubber spatula and fold in the dry ingredients, chocolate chips, and butterscotch chips. Scrape the batter into the prepared pan and smooth into an even layer. Bake until lightly browned and the edges pull away from the sides of the pan, 25 to 30 minutes. Cool completely on a wire rack before cutting into squares or bars.

MAKES SIXTEEN 2 X 3-INCH BARS

Not-Too-Crunchy Granola

Healthy is nice. So is tasty. This crunchy granola is filled with good things and sweetened with brown sugar and maple syrup. A roasting pan beats a baking sheet because its high sides make stirring easier and less messy. As with the Ambrosia on page 234, shaved rather than shredded coconut lends a unique touch to this granola.

ROLLING OVER THE DRIED BANANA SLICES WITH A ROLLING PIN IS A QUICK WAY TO BREAK THEM INTO SPOON-SIZE PIECES. ▶▶

Vegetable oil

3 cups old-fashioned (not quick-cooking) oats

½ cup wheat germ

1 cup slivered almonds

¾ cup shaved unsweetened coconut (optional) (see Sources, page 266)

⅓ cup pure maple syrup

⅓ cup packed light brown sugar

1 cup raisins, dried cherries, or dried cranberries

1 cup dried banana slices, broken into small pieces

1. Place a rack in the center position and preheat the oven to 300°F.

2. Grease a roasting pan generously with vegetable oil. Toss the oats, wheat germ, almonds, and coconut, if using, together in a bowl and spread them out on the roasting pan in an even layer. Bake, stirring two or three times, until lightly browned, about 30 minutes.

3. Whisk together the maple syrup, brown sugar, and 2 tablespoons water in a small bowl until smooth. Drizzle over the oat mixture while stirring. Continue baking, stirring two or three times, until the granola stops forming clumps and the loose oats are light golden brown, about 15 minutes. Remove and stir the raisins and bananas into the pan. Cool completely before storing in an airtight container. The granola will keep for up to 4 weeks.

MAKES ABOUT 6 CUPS

After-Dinner Coffee:
How to Make the Perfect Cup of Java

Back in her salad days—going to college full-time as well as working two jobs to pay her tuition and rent—Susan discovered that coffee was her best friend. And she needed to treat her best friend better than by drinking things like instant coffee. So she did some research and found out how to make the perfect cup of coffee. Here are Susan's tips on the art of coffeemaking:

Buy the freshest beans you can buy. The type of bean I buy—usually arabica that has been French roasted—matters less than the freshness of the roast. (My favorite is Kona, which I fell in love with during a trip to Hawaii with Karl, where he apparently had a fling with the "exotic" front desk attendant. God, you put a lei on that man and you own him forever . . . Maybe that's where I went wrong. Anyway, I'm rambling. On with how to make the perfect cup of coffee.)

- Never freeze the beans. It destroys the flavor.

- Don't use a coffeemaker. The experts recommend the French press, which requires coarser-ground beans but provides a much richer brew than traditional coffeemakers.

- Use a mill to grind the beans. Mill the beans into rough grounds, not too fine—unless you're making espresso, which is an entirely different affair.

- One six-ounce cup of coffee needs two tablespoons of coffee beans. Mix some decaf with the darkest French roast you can find. Make sure to use more decaf. This way it can be "strong" but not caffeine deadly.

- Tap water? Run the faucet for a minute first. If possible, mix bottled in with it.

- While the coffee is brewing, rinse the cups in HOT water. Add milk and let that warm up a little in the cup. Use sugar or whatever sweetener you prefer.

- Pour and rush to a caffeine-deprived friend.

Gabrielle

Gabrielle Solis is first and

foremost a lover of the finest, most expensive things that the world has to offer. Born in a small town to a poor family, it was her goal to be able to afford anything she wanted—and she wanted a lot. She eventually found her way to "the big city," where she became a fashion model and constantly dated the richest men in town. Some may have expected that at dinner with one of these men she would have a salad with skinless chicken or salmon and a Diet Coke, but Gabrielle was luckier than that. She was a size 00 with little effort. As long as she didn't go crazy, she could enjoy all the best foods that men could buy her. It was a life that was easy to get used to—great gourmet food that her date paid for!

When she was in her mid-twenties and realized that modeling jobs were not going to last forever, Gabrielle found a way to make her then-current boyfriend, financier/businessman Carlos Solis, believe that it was *his* idea for them to get married. She knew that with him as her husband she would be set for life. What she didn't know was what that life would bring. Gabrielle never envisioned herself living the picture-perfect life of a suburban housewife. In fact, when she first visited Wisteria Lane with Carlos, she laughed at her soon-to-be-neighbors (including the late Mary Alice Young) for being "victims of Lifetime Television." Less than six months later, she was one of them. And much to her surprise, she actually enjoys it.

Not long after they moved to the neighborhood, Carlos turned his attentions to work and money, and stopped paying enough attention to poor Gabrielle.

She fell into the arms of an eager young gardener . . . But that's a story for another day.

Although Gaby is now most certainly at home on Wisteria Lane, she has never felt at home in her own kitchen. Bree helped her pick out the oversize double stainless steel refrigerator, elaborate gas stove with four burners, and various accessories that fill her well-appointed kitchen, but then was quite disappointed when she found out that Gaby only wanted these nice things so that her kitchen would have that magazine look. She had no intentions of cooking herself. Why do that when you can hire help?

Even the not-so-subtle demands of her late mother-in-law, Juanita (who came home from the market carrying bags of every Spanish and Mexican spice she could find at the local Fairview markets—which, to be fair, was not that many), were lost on Gabrielle, although she was always glad to eat the tasty food Juanita would make.

Left to her own devices, Gabrielle steers toward simple and healthy recipes she can put together on her own. Under duress from Carlos, she might be convinced to help in the creation of some Latin classics.

The following recipes, which are her favorites, are different from the recipes the other women have championed—for these are recipes that Gabrielle would love to cook but won't. And luckily, either with money or with charm, she can always convince someone else to make these fantastic foods for her.

Black Bean Soup

When taking the time to soak and cook the beans isn't an option (and let's face facts, it's never an option when Gabrielle is in the kitchen), here is a more-than-respectable black bean soup that can be on the table in 20 minutes.

FOR THE SOUP

3 cups Chicken Broth (page 37) or store-bought chicken broth

Two 15-ounce cans black beans, drained and rinsed

1 medium yellow onion, finely chopped

One 8-ounce can Goya (or other brand) Spanish-style tomato sauce or 1 cup tomato purée

2 garlic cloves, finely chopped

1 teaspoon ground coriander seed (optional)

½ teaspoon ground cumin

Salt and freshly ground black pepper

OPTIONAL TOPPINGS (USE ANY OR ALL)

Sour cream

Diced red onion

Chopped fresh cilantro

Bottled hot red pepper sauce

1. Combine all the soup ingredients except the salt and pepper in a heavy 3-quart pot. Bring to a boil over medium-high heat. Adjust the heat so the soup is simmering. Cook, uncovered, 15 minutes.

2. Scoop about 1 ½ cups beans and liquid into a blender. Blend at low speed until smooth. Stir back into the soup. Check the seasoning and add salt and pepper to taste. Ladle into warm bowls and pass the toppings separately.

MAKES ABOUT 6 CUPS • SERVES 4 GENEROUSLY

Embrace the pomegranate, although not literally, because the fruit itself is constructed like a large, irregular apple with a leathery shell and is notoriously hard to eat. However, you can embrace the ubiquitous pomegranate juice that is now in the fresh fruit section of your supermarket. Gabrielle can vouch for the qualities of the pomegranate, since during her modeling days, eating the seeds (very high in vitamins C and E and supposedly quite good for the skin) was very much in vogue. Considering that pomegranate juice has three times the antioxidant properties of red wine or green tea, previously regarded as the best protection against heart disease and lifestyle illnesses, this might save your life.

Guacamole with Warm Chips

Sometimes it's the little things—warming chips on a baking sheet in a 200°F oven (or in the warming drawer in the Solis kitchen)—that make a big difference when it comes to food preparation.

1 tablespoon lime juice, or as needed
2 small Hass avocados (about 1 pound)
3 tablespoons minced red onion
2 tablespoons finely chopped fresh cilantro
1 small serrano or ½ jalapeño pepper, cored, seeded, and minced
Salt
Yellow or blue restaurant-style corn chips

Put the lime juice into a medium bowl. Starting at the stem ends, cut through the avocados' skin down to the pit. Work the knife all the way around the pits and twist the two halves to separate them. Flick out the pits with the tip of the knife. Cut each half in half, strip off the peel, and coarsely chop the flesh, adding it to the bowl with the juice. Add the onion, cilantro, and pepper. Mash coarsely with a fork, leaving some largish chunks intact. Add salt to taste. The guacamole can be refrigerated for up to 4 hours. Press a piece of plastic wrap directly to the surface to prevent it from discoloring. Bring to room temperature and let stand for 15 minutes before serving. Spread the chips out in an even layer on a baking sheet and warm in a 250°F oven for 5 minutes. Pile gently into a basket and rewarm as necessary.

MAKES ABOUT 2 CUPS

Gabrielle and Lynette . . .

From: Gabriellemodel@wisterialane.com
To: Lynette.Scavo@wisterialane.com

Lynette,

Last night during our poker game, you asked for my quesadilla recipe. That particular "recipe" involved nothing more than me calling Chef Miguel Arteta at Oaxaca Café and making Carlos pick up the food. That's what I did last night. The only time I went into the kitchen was to remove it from the oven, where I kept it on the warming rack.

However, my late mother-in-law, Juanita, did have a recipe for quesadillas that she would cook from time to time. She was a mean old bat but I can't deny—what she did with cheese and a tortilla was magic!

Love, Gaby

P.S. Carlos seduced our housekeeper, so I kicked him out of the house. Enjoy the quesadillas!

Juanita Solis's Quesadillas

2 cups grated Monterey jack or pepper jack cheese (about 6 ounces)

Four 8-inch flour tortillas

½ cup shredded cooked chicken, drained cooked or canned beans,
  lump crabmeat, or other ingredient (see Note)

2 tablespoons diced roasted red or poblano pepper (either home-roasted
  or store-bought; see box on page 83), optional

Sour cream (optional)

Homemade or store-bought salsa (optional)

Spread the cheese over two of the tortillas, making an even layer that goes right up to the edges of the tortillas. Scatter the chicken, beans, crabmeat, or filling of your choice over the cheese. Do the same with the roasted pepper, if using. Top with the other two tortillas, lining up the edges and pressing them gently into place. The quesadillas can be made up to a day in advance. Put a sheet of paper towel between them and wrap tightly in plastic wrap before refrigerating.

SERVES 4 AS A FIRST COURSE OR 2 AS A MAIN COURSE

Note: Just about any solid slightly-smaller-than-bite-size ingredient can be used. Chopped red onions, cooked in a pan with a little oil until well browned, are delicious. So are chopped shrimp, shredded meat from leftover barbecued spareribs, chopped cooked vegetables or mushrooms, or coarsely chopped leftover beef steak.

Cooking and Serving Quesadillas

Just as quesadillas can be filled in many ways, they can also be cooked in many ways. Here are a few. It's best to let the quesadillas stand a few minutes before serving—the molten filling will cool slightly, making them easier to cut and eat. Cut each quesadilla into quarters and top each wedge with a dollop of sour cream and a spoonful of salsa (or pass the sour cream and salsa separately).

To Grill the Quesadillas:

Light a gas grill or start a charcoal fire. Either way, the grill is ready when you can hold the palm of your hand about 1 inch above the grill for 3 to 4 seconds before having to move it. Grill the quesadillas until the underside is golden brown in spots and grill marked, about 4 minutes. Flip and repeat.

To Panfry the Quesadillas:

Lightly oil a flat-bottomed heavy pan (cast iron is ideal) with a paper towel dipped in vegetable oil. Heat over medium heat a few minutes. The pan is ready when a few drops of water flicked into the pan dance for 2 to 3 seconds before evaporating. Slip one of the quesadillas into the pan and cook until the underside is spotty golden brown, 4 to 5 minutes. Carefully flip and cook the second side in the same way. Repeat with the second quesadilla. If you have a griddle, heat it over two burners and cook both quesadillas at the same time. (Set an electric griddle to 350°F.)

To Broil the Quesadillas:

Set a rack about 5 inches from the broiler and preheat the broiler to low. Put the quesadillas on a baking sheet and broil until the top side is golden brown and the cheese starts to melt. Flip the quesadillas and cook the second side in the same way. Rotate the sheet as necessary to brown the quesadillas evenly.

The ABCs of Quesadillas

Quesadillas are nothing more than two tortillas enclosing grated cheese and any number of other ingredients. These "sandwiches" are then cooked to crisp up the tortillas and heat the filling. Usually the tortillas are made with white flour (corn tortillas don't quite cut it here), but whole-wheat tortillas are becoming increasingly available in many markets. Use them if you like. Choose a good melting cheese, like Monterey jack, for the filling. After that, the sky's the limit.

Spicy Paella

The one dish from childhood that Gabrielle will occasionally prepare herself is a simple recipe that allows one to make paella without a special paella pan. This is the same dish that Gaby prepared for Mary Alice Young's wake.

½ cup dry white wine

1 teaspoon saffron threads

3 tablespoons olive oil

6 boneless, skinless chicken thighs (about 1 ½ pounds), cut into rough 1 ½-inch pieces

3 links spicy chorizo, cut into ½-inch slices (about ¾ pound)

1 medium yellow onion, cut into ½-inch dice (about 1 ¼ cups)

1 medium red bell pepper, cored, seeded, and cut into ½-inch dice (about 1 cup)

½ teaspoon cayenne pepper (optional)

Salt and freshly ground black pepper

1 ½ cups Uncle Ben's rice

3 cups Chicken Broth (page 37) or store-bought chicken broth

1 pound large shrimp, peeled and deveined (about 20 per pound)

24 mussels

12 littleneck or other hard-shell clams

1 cup frozen peas

1. Pour the wine over the saffron in a small bowl. Let stand while preparing the paella.

2. Heat the olive oil in a wide, deep (at least 12 inches wide by 3 inches deep), heavy casserole over medium heat. Add the chicken and chorizo. Cook, turning as necessary, until the chicken is lightly browned on all sides, about 8 minutes. With a slotted spoon, scoop the chicken and chorizo into a bowl.

3. Add the onion, red pepper, and cayenne, if using, to the pan. Season lightly with salt and pepper. Cook, stirring, until the vegetables are wilted, about 6 minutes. Stir in the rice and cook a minute or two. Pour in the saffron mixture and cook, stirring, until the liquid evaporates. Stir the chicken and chorizo into the rice.

CONTINUED

Pour in the broth and bring to a boil. Season generously with salt and pepper. The amount will depend on the broth. Boil until the level of broth reaches the rice.

4. Scatter the shrimp, mussels, and clams over the rice, stir into the rice thoroughly, and reduce the heat to medium-low. Cover the casserole and cook until the broth is absorbed and the rice is tender, about 15 minutes.

5. Scatter the peas over the rice, stir them in, and serve right away, including some of each ingredient and some rice with each serving.

SERVES 6

Sunset Chicken and Rice

The combination of turmeric and tomato sauce gives this dish a deep orange glow. Converted rice cooks differently from regular long-grain rice. It is a little more forgiving in dishes like this, where long-grain rice might cook unevenly.

One 3½-pound chicken, cut into 8 pieces
Salt and freshly ground black pepper
2 tablespoons vegetable oil
I large onion, finely chopped
2 garlic cloves, finely chopped
1 teaspoon turmeric
½ cup dry white wine
3 cups Chicken Broth (page 37) or store-bought chicken broth
One 8-ounce can Spanish-style tomato sauce
1 bay leaf
1 cup frozen peas, preferably not baby peas
One 8-ounce jar bottled chopped pimientos, drained (about ½ cup)
2 cups Uncle Ben's rice

1. Cut the chicken breasts in half crosswise with a heavy knife. Blot the chicken pieces dry with paper towels and season them liberally with salt and pepper. Heat the oil in a 12-inch-wide Dutch oven or flameproof casserole over medium heat until rippling. Add the chicken to the pot, skin-side down. Cook, turning, until browned on all sides, about 15 minutes. Transfer the chicken pieces to a plate.

2. Spoon off all but 2 tablespoons of fat from the pan. Add the onion, garlic, and turmeric to the pot and cook, stirring, until lightly browned, about 6 minutes. Stir in the white wine and bring to a boil, scraping up the brown bits that are stuck to the pan. Stir in the broth, tomato sauce, and bay leaf. Return the chicken to the pot. Add the peas and pimientos, then the rice. Wiggle the pot by its handles to settle the rice into an even layer below the surface of the liquid. Bring to a boil, then adjust the heat so the liquid is barely simmering. Cover the pot and cook until the rice is tender and the chicken is cooked through, about 25 minutes. Give everything a big stir, re-cover the pot, and let stand 5 minutes before serving.

BROWN THE CHICKEN SLOWLY AND STEADILY. THE CHICKEN SHOULD BE ABOUT HALF COOKED AT THE END OF BROWN-ING. IF THE CHICKEN IS BROWNING TOO FAST, TURN DOWN THE HEAT.

SERVES 4

GABRIELLE'S SHOPPING LIST

Dear Xiao-Mei,
Please pick up the following:

Essentials
Bubble bath
Scented candles
Teen People magazine
Ice
Dom Perignon

Whipped cream
Condoms
Merlot (2 bottles)
Tequila (Añejo)

In Case There's Time
Crabcakes
Tortilla chips
Salsa
avocados
Filet mignon
Shrimp cocktail
Polenta
Bruschetta
Baguette
French bread
Habaneros
Jalapeños
Clif bars
Smoothie makings
Soy milk

protein powder
cereal
orange juice
eggs
bacon
frozen tamales
Carne asada
Corn tortillas
onions
pork loin
Cumin
bell peppers
Cholula hot sauce
black beans
White rice

Tamales

Tamales are not difficult to prepare, but they do take a little time. If you rope a family member into helping, things will move along quickly. And it's a good way to keep an eye on them, too.

Dried cornhusks (see Notes)

FOR THE MASA (CORNMEAL DOUGH)

3 cups masa for tamales, such as Maseca brand
  (see Notes on page 149 and Sources on page 266)
1 ½ teaspoons salt (less if using canned broth)
½ teaspoon baking powder
2 cups Chicken Broth (page 37) or store-bought chicken broth
¾ cup vegetable oil

FOR THE CHICKEN FILLING

2 tablespoons vegetable oil
1 small yellow onion, cut into ½-inch dice (about ¾ cup)
3 tablespoons canned diced chilies or 2 serrano chilies, cored,
  seeded, and finely chopped
1 cup coarsely chopped or shredded cooked chicken or turkey
Salt

Hot red pepper sauce (optional)

1. Prepare the cornhusks: Dried cornhusks are usually flat along one edge and tapered at the opposite edge. Husks that measure between 8 and 9 inches from top to bottom and from side to side are best. Larger husks can be trimmed (after soaking) and smaller husks can be overlapped to make enough surface area. Count out 15 husks of the right size (a few for margin of error). Ruffle them to separate them slightly and set them in a very large bowl. Pour in enough cool water to cover them completely. Weight them down below the surface of the water with a plate and let soak until pliable, about 1 hour.

CONTINUED

2. Make the masa: Stir the masa for tamales, salt, and baking powder together in the bowl of an electric mixer. Heat the broth in a small saucepan over low heat until steam rises from the top. Remove from the heat and stir in the vegetable oil. Pour the broth mixture into the dry ingredients and beat at low speed until smooth and slightly shiny, about 3 minutes. (You can also mix the masa by hand: Stir the liquid and dry ingredients together in a large bowl with a wooden spoon until mixed. Then beat like heck until smooth and shiny or your arm gives out.) Set aside while making the chicken filling.

3. Make the chicken filling: Heat the oil in a medium skillet over medium heat until rippling. Add the onion and cook, stirring, until softened, about 5 minutes. Add the chilies and cook, stirring, until the onion starts to brown, a minute or two. Scrape into a mixing bowl, add the chicken, and stir to mix well. Season to taste with salt.

4. Form the tamales: Cut a dozen 10-inch lengths of kitchen twine. Drain the husks. Spread one out on a work surface. Use about ⅓ cup (slightly more for larger husks, slightly less for smaller ones) of the masa to form a rectangle about 3 inches long by 2 inches wide in the center of the husk. Make a deep indentation with your thumb in the center of the masa and fill the indentation with a rounded tablespoon of the chicken filling. Fold the top and bottom of the husk over the filling, then, one at a time, fold the sides over the filling to form a compact packet. Don't make the packets too tight; they will expand during cooking. Tie a length of twine around the center of the packet to keep the ends in place. Set aside. Once you get the hang of it, you can fill a few of them at a time to move things along.

5. Set up a steamer (see box on page 150). Arrange the tamales in a single layer and cook until the filling is fully cooked, about 1 hour. Check the water in the bottom of the steamer several times during cooking and replenish if necessary.

6. To serve: Pile the cooked tamales on a platter. Pass the platter around, letting people help themselves and unwrap their own tamales. Pass hot red pepper sauce separately, if you like.

MAKES 12 TAMALES (THE RECIPE CAN BE EASILY DOUBLED)

Dried cornhusks are available in Latin markets, some specialty stores, and from many online vendors. (See Sources, page 266.)

Masa is a confusing word to those who don't speak Spanish, as well as to some who do. Masa can mean meal (as in ground grain) or a dough made from that meal or from flour. For tamales, be sure to use packaged ground corn labeled *masa para tamales* (flour for tamales) and not plain cornmeal (labeled *harina de maiz*). The former contains a bit of lime, which is essential to a light and spongy filling.

Steamers

Many types of steamers, ranging in price from very inexpensive to expensive, are available in cookware stores. On the lower end of the price range are bamboo steamers, sold in many Asian markets, and the collapsible type of stainless steel steamer that unfolds to fit inside shallow casseroles or wide saucepans. In either case, buy the largest one that will fit over your widest wok or into your widest pot. Some cookware sets include a steamer insert that (usually) fits into the largest pot in the set.

Regardless of type, the method is the same. Set the steamer over (not touching) boiling water and make sure the lid of the steamer or pot it fits into can close tightly. Lay the foods to be steamed into the steamer in a single layer, if possible, and cover the steamer. In the case of long-steaming items, like tamales, check the water occasionally to make sure it hasn't boiled away.

Green Rice

Extracting exotic flavors from simple ingredients is a good way to use odds and ends of bunches of cilantro, parsley, or scallions. The texture of this beautiful rice is more creamy than fluffy. The flavor is at home with anything from curry to grilled pork chops.

About 2 cups Chicken Broth (page 37) or store-bought chicken broth
½ cup packed fresh Italian parsley leaves
4 scallions, trimmed, whites cut into ¼-inch slices, greens coarsely chopped
¼ cup lightly packed cilantro leaves
2 tablespoons unsalted butter
2 cups long-grain rice
One 13 ½-ounce can coconut milk or "light" coconut milk
   (available in gourmet markets, Asian and Latin markets,
   and online; see Sources, page 266)
Salt

1. Pour 1 cup of broth into a blender. Add the parsley, scallion greens, and cilantro and blend at low speed until the liquid turns a vivid green and the herbs and scallion greens are finely chopped. Pour into a 2-cup measure and add enough broth to measure 2 cups.

2. Heat the butter in a heavy 2-quart saucepan over medium heat. Add the scallion whites and cook, stirring, until lightly browned, about 3 minutes. Add the rice and stir until coated with butter. Pour in the green broth and coconut milk and bring to a boil over high heat. Add salt to taste, reduce the heat to medium-low, and cover the pot. Cook until the rice is tender, about 18 minutes. Remove from the heat and let stand, covered, 3 minutes. Stir with a fork and serve.

SERVES 6

Mexican Hot Chocolate

Mexico—the birthplace of chocolate drinks—gives us sweetened chocolate flavored with cinnamon. The most readily available brand, Ibarra, comes in a brightly colored six-sided box (see Sources, page 266). See the Note below if you'd like to substitute regular chocolate for its Mexican counterpart.

In Mexico, a special wooden tool called a *molinillo* is used to make a frothy cupful. The *molinillo*, which consists of one or more wooden rings kept in place between two decoratively notched wooden balls on a long stick, is immersed in the chocolate and rotated between the palms of your hands until the chocolate is frothy. A metal whisk or immersion blender works just fine.

PER SERVING

½ disc Mexican chocolate (about 1 ½ ounces;
   see Note below and Sources on page 266)
1 cup milk

Cut the chocolate into wedges along the indentations. Place them and the milk in a deep saucepan. Heat over low heat until the chocolate is softened and the milk is steaming. Whisk (or blend with an immersion blender) until the chocolate is completely dissolved and the liquid is frothy. Pour into a mug and serve immediately.

Note: If Mexican chocolate is unavailable, substitute 1 ½ squares (1 ½ ounces) semisweet baking chocolate and ¼ teaspoon ground cinnamon. Proceed as above.

Bloody Marias

G abrielle's spin on the traditional Bloody Mary, this is an excellent drink for weekend relaxation, dinner parties, or even an afternoon tryst. But if you're doing the latter, be sure to clean up afterward: The ingredients are pretty conspicuous.

FOR THE MIX

1 quart tomato or V-8 juice

3 tablespoons lime juice

3 tablespoons bottled horseradish

2 teaspoons Worcestershire sauce

1 teaspoon hot red pepper sauce, plus more for passing around

1 ½ teaspoons toasted and ground celery seed (see box below)
   or 1 teaspoon celery salt

Drained juice from Salsa Piccante (page 167), optional, but very nice

PER DRINK

Ice

1 ½ to 2 ounces tequila

⅔ cup Bloody Maria mix

Medium celery stalks with leaves, trimmed, washed, and cut in half
   lengthwise, or cucumber spears made by cutting whole cucumbers
   lengthwise into wedges

1. Make the mix: Stir all mix ingredients together in a pitcher large enough to hold them comfortably and chill.

2. Per drink: Fill a glass with ice and pour in the tequila. Fill with mix and stick in a celery stalk or cucumber spear.

MAKES 5 CUPS, ENOUGH FOR 8 DRINKS

I f you have a small electric spice grinder, try this flavor hit: Toast the celery seeds in a small skillet over low heat until they are fragrant. Cool completely, then grind to a powder. The difference is inspiring.

Gabrielle on Guilty Pleasure

Sorry to disappoint you, but Gabrielle's favorite guilty pleasure is a little snack she had when her family spent a week in South Carolina. It's not exotic. It's certainly not Spanish-infused or Mexican. It's something altogether surprising, although certainly not sensual.

Boiled peanuts.

I know. I know. It sounds awful. But once you get over the fact that peanuts are the main ingredient, you'll realize that these are not the peanuts you get at the park, the ballgame, or the circus. This regional delicacy is like something you've never tasted before.

Throughout the South, boiled peanuts are sold at roadside stands and local restaurants. If you want the best-tasting ones, however, check the kitchens of the people who live in the Carolinas.

Peanuts boiled in the shell with lots of salt taste like edamame (soybeans, to those unfamiliar with Japanese cuisine)—which isn't surprising, since both peanuts and soybeans are legumes, not nuts. Peanuts are actually part of the legume family—think peas and beans—*not* the nut family.

Mrs. O'Leary

For over 130 years, popular opinion has been that Mrs. O'Leary's cow started the Great Chicago Fire. No empirical evidence exists to cement this housewife's guilt. No admissions were ever made. Nothing was ever proven. Only one fact is not subject to debate: On the evening of October 8, 1871, a fire started on DeKoven Street in Chicago. This fire went on to burn a large percentage of the city, an event known as the Great Chicago Fire. Over 300 people died, and more than 17,000 buildings and over 2,000 acres of land were destroyed.

The story of Mrs. O'Leary and her bovine companion originated with a story in the *Chicago Evening Journal*, where the fire was described as being started by her cow Daisy. Daisy allegedly kicked over a lamp in the stable in which she was being milked. For some reason, this story stuck and the once content and happy Mrs. O'Leary never recovered from the accusation, becoming a most desperate housewife in the process.

Despite detailed evidence to the contrary and numerous reasons for the massive destruction the fire wrought on the city of Chicago (unusually dry conditions, substandard fire hoses, wooden structures, poor communication between the firefighters), Mrs. O'Leary was perceived as the cause of the fire. Perhaps the enduring nature of the legend is attributable to the fact that Mrs. O'Leary was such a malleable figure, a woman who could be used to discover and express different and even conflicting meanings. From the outset, people were not interested in knowing the real Catherine O'Leary. She was alternately old and haggard, pretty and hardworking, stout and unpleasant—any personality one wanted to superimpose on her seemed to be acceptable.

More than a hundred years later, things have not changed. Poor Mrs. O'Leary is still the scapegoat for a terrible tragedy. From the 1938 movie *In Old Chicago* to the more recent Brian Wilson song "Mrs. O'Leary's Cow," this desperate housewife's guilt seems to be ingrained in the public consciousness. Mrs. O'Leary denied the charges from her deathbed in 1885, claiming she and her husband were in bed when the fire started. One hopes Daisy was not at the scene.

Mrs. O'Leary's
Spiked Baked Custards

2 large eggs plus 2 yolks

⅓ cup sugar

2 tablespoons Bailey's Irish Cream liqueur

¼ teaspoon salt

1 cup heavy cream

1 ½ cups milk (or 2 ½ cups milk and omit the cream)

1. Set a rack in the center position and preheat the oven to 325°F. Fill a teakettle with water and bring it to a boil.

2. Beat the eggs, yolks, sugar, Bailey's, and salt in a mixing bowl with a whisk just until blended. Pour the cream and milk (or all milk) into the bowl slowly, whisking constantly. If necessary, stir until the sugar is dissolved.

3. Divide the egg mixture among four 8-ounce ramekins or custard cups. Put them in a baking dish just large enough to hold them comfortably. Place the dish on the oven rack and pour in enough boiling water to come halfway up the sides of the ramekins. Bake until all but about 1 inch in the center of the custards wiggles when the cup is shaken gently, about 35 minutes. (The very centers of the custards will seem liquidy; they will set as the custard cools.)

4. Remove the baking pan from the oven and cool the custards in the water bath to room temperature. Refrigerate the cooled custards until set—at least 4 hours or up to 2 days —before serving.

SERVES 4

From Gabrielle's modeling days, she learned to eat a very simple diet. Here are a few simple recipes that she liked back in the day. (We'll leave out the *jambon avec beurre* on baguettes, which was her favorite dish when doing the pret-à-porter shows in Paris and Milan, for obvious reasons.)

Fruit Salad with Yogurt-Honey Dressing

Honeydew, cantaloupe, pineapple, and some other fruits are now widely available already peeled and cut into serving-size pieces. Using a few of those, this salad can be on the table in 5 minutes.

FOR THE SALAD (PICK ANY 3 OF THE FOLLOWING)

1 ripe small (Hawaiian) papaya, halved, seeded, peeled, and cut into 1-inch pieces (about 2 cups)

2 cups pineapple, cut into 1-inch pieces

One 1-pint basket strawberries, hulled, and cut in half if large

2 cups honeydew or cantaloupe melons, cut into 1-inch pieces

2 tangerines, peeled and pulled apart into segments

4 kiwis, peeled, cut in half lengthwise, then into ½-inch slices

FOR THE DRESSING

1 cup vanilla yogurt

¼ cup orange juice

1 ½ tablespoons honey

1 tablespoon poppy seeds

Toasted sliced almonds (see tip for toasting walnuts on page 251)

1. Toss the fruits of your choice together gently in a large bowl. In a separate bowl, whisk the yogurt, orange juice, honey, and poppy seeds together until blended.

2. Mound the fruit onto serving plates. Drizzle the dressing over and around the fruit and scatter the almonds over the top.

SERVES 6

Sweet and Tangy Chicken Stir-Fry

I f all the ingredients are measured and assembled beforehand (as they should be), this stir-fry is so quick that you can make a pot of rice and remove it from the heat before starting the stir-fry. The rice will stay nice and hot until the chicken is ready.

3 tablespoons orange juice

1 tablespoon soy sauce

1 teaspoon sugar

¾ pound boneless, skinless chicken breast, cut into ½-inch-wide strips

1 teaspoon toasted sesame oil or hot sesame oil (optional)

1 tablespoon vegetable oil

3 scallions, trimmed and minced

1 tablespoon minced fresh ginger

3 garlic cloves, minced

1 celery stalk, trimmed and cut on the bias into ¼-inch slices
(about ½ cup)

¼ pound snow peas, ends removed and cut in half crosswise
(about 1 ½ cups)

1. Stir the orange juice, soy sauce, and sugar together in a small bowl until the sugar is dissolved. Pat the chicken pieces dry with paper towels. Toss them in a bowl with the sesame oil, if using, until coated.

2. Heat the vegetable oil in a heavy, large (12-inch) nonstick skillet over high heat until the oil is rippling and thin. Add the scallions, ginger, and garlic to the pan and cook, stirring, until you can smell the garlic. Add the chicken and cook, tossing, until lightly browned on all sides, about 2 minutes. Add the celery and snow peas and cook, tossing, until the snow peas turn bright green.

3. Pour the soy sauce mixture into the pan, bring to a boil, and cook, tossing, until the liquid is boiled down to a glaze thick enough to coat the chicken and vegetables. Serve immediately.

SERVES 2

Chicken (or Shrimp) Curry in a Hurry

Serve with plain boiled rice or the Green Rice on page 151. To make the shrimp variation, substitute shrimp for chicken and proceed as below, shaving a minute off the browning and the final simmering to prevent overcooking the shrimp.

3 scallions, trimmed and cut into 2-inch lengths

2 garlic cloves

3 quarter-size slices peeled fresh ginger

1 chili pepper, hot, hotter, or hottest (jalapeño, serrano, or Scotch bonnet, respectively), cut in half, stem, core, and seeds removed

¾ pound boneless chicken breasts, cut into 1 ½-inch pieces, or ¾ pound large shrimp, peeled and deveined (about 16 shrimp)

Salt and freshly ground black pepper

All-purpose flour

2 tablespoons vegetable oil

1 large yellow onion, thinly sliced

1 medium red bell pepper, cored, seeded, and cut into very thin strips

1 tablespoon curry powder

½ cup Chicken Broth (page 37) or store-bought chicken broth

¼ cup canned coconut milk or "light" coconut milk (available in gourmet markets, Asian and Latin markets, and online; see Sources, page 266)

1. Put the scallions, garlic, ginger, and chili in a small food processor and process until very finely chopped. Scrape into a small bowl and set aside.

2. Season the chicken pieces with salt and pepper. Spread the flour out on a plate and toss the chicken pieces in it until coated. Bounce the chicken around in your hands to remove as much flour as possible and put the chicken on a clean plate.

3. Heat the oil in a large (12-inch) nonstick skillet over medium-high heat until rippling. Add the chicken and toss/turn until lightly browned on all sides, about 4 minutes. Scatter the onion, red pepper, and ginger-garlic mix over the chicken and toss until blended. Sprinkle the curry powder over everything and toss until the onion and pepper are wilted, about 2 minutes. Pour in the broth and coconut milk. Bring to a boil, stirring, and cook until the chicken is cooked through and the sauce is boiling and lightly thickened, about 2 minutes. Serve hot.

SERVES 2

Shrimp with Chorizo and Bell Pepper

Chorizos are a deep red sausage found in one form or another all across the Spanish-speaking world. Like people, chorizos come in all sizes, shapes, and degrees of spice. Most are fully cooked, so all they need is a little toss in a pan to warm them. Here they add color, flavor, and a little heat to a simple dish of sweet shrimp and crispy red peppers. Serve with plain or Green Rice (see page 151) and dinner can be on the table in 20 minutes.

1 small yellow or red bell pepper

2 tablespoons olive oil

3 garlic cloves, thinly sliced

1 link chorizo (about 4 ounces), as mild or spicy as you like,
    cut into ½-inch slices, then into ½-inch strips

16 very large shrimp, peeled, tails removed, and deveined (about ¾ pound)

3 tablespoons sherry or dry white wine

1 large tomato, peeled, seeded, and diced (see page 48)

3 scallions, trimmed and cut into 1-inch lengths

2 tablespoons finely chopped fresh parsley, cilantro, or chives

1 tablespoon butter (optional)

1. Cut the pepper in half through the stem. Pull out the stem, core, and seeds. Cut the pepper halves in half, then into very thin strips, and set aside.

2. Heat the oil in a 10- to 11-inch skillet over medium heat until rippling. Add the garlic and cook, shaking the pan, until the garlic is sizzling. Stir in the chorizo and stir-toss until the chorizo changes color and the oil picks up color from the chorizo, about 3 minutes.

3. Increase the heat to high, add the shrimp and pepper strips, and cook, stirring, until the shrimp are bright pink and almost cooked through, about 3 minutes. The shrimp should give off a lively sizzle and the bits that stick to the pan should turn a rich brown but not blacken.

4. Pour in the wine, reduce the heat to medium, and cook, scraping the bottom of the pan, until the wine is mostly evaporated and the shrimp are cooked through, about 2 minutes. Add the tomato, scallions, and herb of choice and toss well. Remove the pan from the heat and stir in the butter. Serve immediately.

SERVES 2 (INGREDIENTS CAN BE EASILY DOUBLED TO SERVE 4;
USE A 12-INCH SKILLET.)

Penne with Spiced Vodka Sauce

This is a classic of the restaurant world that made a simple shift into home kitchens. This version is given a kick with crushed red pepper and a touch of freshness with basil. It is nice made with penne rigati but is fine with regular penne as well.

STRAINED TOMA-
TOES, AVAILABLE
IN "STERILE-PACK"
CONTAINERS, ARE
LIGHTER AND
FRESHER TASTING
THAN CANNED
TOMATO PURÉE.
IF CANNED PURÉE
IS ALL YOU CAN
FIND, USE 1 CUP
PURÉE THINNED
WITH ½ CUP
WATER.

Salt

2 tablespoons olive oil

2 garlic cloves, minced

½ teaspoon crushed hot red pepper, or less

¼ cup vodka

1 ¼ cups strained tomatoes

½ cup light cream

¾ pound penne rigati or regular penne (about 4 ½ cups)

12 large fresh basil leaves, cut crosswise into thin strips

½ cup grated Parmesan cheese

1 ½ cups fresh mozzarella, cut in ½-inch dice (optional)

1. Bring a large pot of salted water to a boil.

2. Meanwhile, heat the olive oil in a large skillet. Add the garlic and hot pepper and cook, shaking the pan, just until you can smell the garlic. Remove the pan from the heat and pour in the vodka—carefully; even off the heat it may ignite. When the boiling stops, return the pan to the heat and stir in the strained tomatoes. Season lightly with salt. Bring to a simmer, adjust the heat so the sauce is simmering, and cook 5 minutes. (The sauce can be prepared to this point up to 2 days in advance. Refrigerate and reheat to simmering before continuing.) Turn off the heat and stir in the cream.

3. Stir the penne into the boiling water. Cook, stirring occasionally, until tender but still firm (there should be a slight ring of white in the center of the penne when one is bitten into). Reserve ½ cup of the cooking liquid and drain the pasta.

CONTINUED

4. Return the penne to the pot, scrape in the sauce, and add the basil. Stir over low heat, adding some of the reserved liquid, if necessary, to make a sauce that lightly coats the pasta. Taste and add salt if necessary. Remove from the heat and stir in the Parmesan and the mozzarella, if using. Serve from a platter or ladle into warm shallow bowls.

SERVES 4

Salsa Piccante

S alsa is best if served without refrigerating, but it can be made up to a day in advance if need be. Drain the salsa before serving with chips, but leave it in the juice if serving with poultry, meat, or fish. Save the incredibly flavorful juices for Bloody Marias (page 154) or to season dressings or soups.

1 large ripe tomato (about ¾ pound) or 3 ripe medium
   plum tomatoes
¼ cup minced red onion
¼ cup finely chopped cilantro
1 medium or 2 small serrano peppers, cored, seeded,
   and finely chopped
Salt

1. Cut the cores from the tomato(es). Set cored-side down, and cut into ¼-inch slices from top to bottom. Cut the slices into ¼-inch dice. Scrape the tomatoes and their juice into a mixing bowl. Add the onion, cilantro, and chilies. Toss well and season lightly with salt to taste. Let stand 30 minutes or so.

2. Check the salt and add more if necessary. Drain or not, according to how you are serving the salsa (see headnote).

MAKES ABOUT 2 CUPS

Rum-Glazed Roasted Pineapple

With the advent of fresh pineapple being sold in supermarkets in an already peeled and cored state, the prep for this simple dessert is a done deal. Roasted pineapple is delicious on its own, sprinkled with toasted sesame seeds, or served alongside vanilla ice cream.

Vegetable oil
3 cups peeled and cored pineapple in roughly 2-inch pieces
2 tablespoons dark brown sugar
1 tablespoon butter, melted
1 tablespoon rum, preferably dark

1. Place a rack in the highest position and preheat the oven to 450°F. Lightly grease an 8 x 11-inch baking dish with vegetable oil.

2. In a bowl, toss the pineapple together with the sugar, butter, and rum until the pineapple is coated. Spread out in an even layer in the prepared dish, scraping the liquid from the bowl into the pan, and set the bowl aside. Roast, turning the pieces two or three times, until the pineapple is coated with a deep golden brown glaze, about 25 minutes. Scrape the pineapple and any glaze from the pan into the bowl. Toss to coat. Serve warm or room temperature.

SERVES 4

Toasted Angel Food Cake with Spiced Strawberries

This is a guilt-free dessert in the form of toasted angel food cake with a sweet and subtly spiced strawberry compote.

1 pint ripe juicy strawberries
1 tablespoon sugar, or as needed
½ teaspoon lemon juice, or as needed
¼ teaspoon ground ginger
3 grinds of black pepper

Four 1-inch slices homemade or store-bought angel food cake
Melted butter (optional)

1. Wash the strawberries, drain them, and pat them dry. Cut out the hulls and cut the berries in quarters, dropping them in a bowl as you go. Add the sugar, lemon juice, ginger, and pepper. Let stand at room temperature, tossing occasionally, 1 to 2 hours. Taste and add more lemon juice and/or sugar if you like.

2. To serve: Set a rack about 5 inches from the broiler and heat the broiler to low. Set the cake slices close together (for more even broiling) on a baking sheet. Brush the tops very lightly with butter, if you like. Broil until golden brown, about 2 minutes. Flip and repeat. Serve warm, spooning some of the strawberries over the cake and passing the rest separately.

SERVES 4

Pineapple-Peach Smoothie

¾ cup pineapple juice or juice reserved from crushed pineapple
   (see Pineapple-Bran Muffins, page 63)

1 ½ cups frozen sliced peaches

½ cup vanilla or plain soy milk

½ teaspoon pure vanilla extract (if using plain soy milk)

Blend the pineapple juice and peaches at low speed until the peaches are finely chopped. Increase the speed to high and, with the motor running, pour the soy milk (and vanilla if using) into the blender. Blend until smooth and frothy. Pour into a cold glass and drink right away.

MAKES 1 LARGE OR 2 SMALL DRINKS

Lynette

Pragmatic is the first word

that comes to mind when asked to describe Lynette Scavo. Mother of four and wife of perennial nice guy Tom, Lynette is an intelligent, strong-willed woman who, more often than not, will do most anything to get what she wants.

This is most evident with regard to her life as a wife and mother. Things are not always easy in the Scavo household. A successful businesswoman turned stay-at-home mother turned successful businesswoman *and* mother, Lynette sometimes forgets to leave the business mind-set at the office.

Whether it's in the kitchen or the bedroom, she performs with ruthless efficiency and can rub people the wrong way with her (sometimes too) truthful comments. But this same blunt honesty also makes her a valuable friend to her fellow desperate housewives on Wisteria Lane. For there is no one else willing to call them out on their weaknesses, failures, or deceptions—even if this can sometimes get Lynette into trouble. (She was one of the first to call Bree on her alcohol problem, even though Bree, at the time, was unwilling to deal with it.)

From handling her advertising accounts, to dealing with Tom's behavior in the office and at home (not to mention the bedroom), to finding time to be a good mother to Parker, Porter, Preston, and Penny, Lynette's picture should be in the dictionary under the word *multi-tasker*. Of course, all this work leaves little time for exotic dishes and fine cuisine. These days, this housewife is usually grateful if she's able to cook a meal instead of picking up takeout on the way home from the office.

Like most people, Lynette has a complicated relationship with food. Her goals in the kitchen are practical ones. She yearns to find a way to make sure her family eats healthy, good-quality meals, but knows that she doesn't really have the time to prepare them on a nightly basis. She prefers food she can prep the night before and toss into the oven after work to elaborate feasts that require hours in the kitchen in order to ensure that the meal is "just so."

When she has the time, Lynette loves making her favorite recipes. She craves her specialty dishes—her family's recipe for Buttermilk-Soaked Fried Chicken, with her famous Potato Casserole and Glazed Brussels Sprouts (the sort the kids hate), is her personal favorite. She also enjoys making simple time-tested meals like her Old-School Buttered Noodles.

Lynette also enjoys a nice romantic dinner from time to time. On the rare occasion that she has enough free time to cook one, she excels at it, bringing her level of discipline and perfection to the kitchen the same way she brings it to the office. Unfortunately, Tom has not always been fully appreciative of her efforts in the past. (This was more the case when Lynette was a stay-at-home mom and Tom was the breadwinner.)

Since they have switched roles several times—both having experienced being the stay-at-home parent and the sole breadwinner—Tom has grown to greatly appreciate the value of Lynette's rare excursion into the kitchen to prepare a romantic dinner.

Whether she's spent the day taking care of the kids or climbing the corporate ladder, when it's time to make the kids' lunch or put a family dinner on the table, Lynette will take quick over perfect. On the rare nights she and Tom can settle in for a romantic dinner, or when she's entertaining clients, Lynette's passion for perfection and penchant for planning shine through.

Everything You Always Wanted to Know About Grilled Cheese (But Were Too Busy to Ask)

Everyone knows how to make a grilled cheese sandwich, but not everyone knows how to make a perfect one. Longer, slow cooking makes for delectably crunchy bread and thoroughly melted cheese. It's the perfect family meal for the Scavos, since everyone—save Penny, who still needs a few more teeth—loves Lynette's grilled cheese.

PER SANDWICH

> 2 slices wheat or white bread
> 3 slices easily melted cheese, such as American, Muenster, or white Cheddar (about 2 ounces)
> 1 tablespoon softened butter or olive oil

OPTIONAL FILLINGS (PICK ONE)

> 3 slices bacon, cooked until crisp
> 3 thin slices tomato (less than ¼-inch)
> 2 thin slices ham or smoked turkey

Heat a heavy, flat—cast iron is perfect—skillet or griddle over medium-low heat. Make the sandwiches, placing one of the optional fillings, if using, between the slices of cheese, not next to the bread.

BUTTER METHOD:

Spread the butter over both sides of the sandwich, dividing it evenly. Set the bread into the skillet; there should be barely a sizzle. Cook until crisp and deep golden brown. This should take a full 4 to 5 minutes. If the sandwich is browning faster than that, lower the heat. Flip and repeat.

CONTINUED

OLIVE OIL METHOD:

Pour enough olive oil into the skillet or onto the griddle to make a thin, even film. Grill the sandwiches as in the butter method, but lift the sandwich and replenish the oil before flipping.

Here are dressed-up ideas for an everyday favorite. If butter is your grilling medium of choice, any grilled cheese sandwich can be dressed up by pressing herb leaves onto the butter before grilling. Match the herb to the filling: perhaps parsley for a plain grilled cheese, basil for a grilled cheese and tomato, or cilantro for the grilled pepper jack and chicken below.

Each makes 1 sandwich.

Sun-dried Tomato Goat Cheese:

Beat ¼ cup softened goat cheese with 2 tablespoons finely chopped sun-dried tomatoes (soaked and drained if necessary) until smooth. Season liberally with freshly ground black pepper. Spread over one slice of bread, top with another, and grill as directed on pages 175 and 176.

Smoked Gouda and Mushroom:

Toss ½ cup coarsely grated smoked Gouda and ¼ cup coarsely chopped cooked mushrooms together in a small bowl. Pile onto one slice of bread, top with another, and grill as directed on pages 175 and 176.

Pepper Jack and Chicken:

Toss ½ cup coarsely grated pepper jack cheese and ⅓ cup shredded cooked chicken (or turkey) together in a small bowl. Pile onto one slice of bread, top with another, and grill as directed on pages 175 and 176.

Warm Turkey, Muenster, and Coleslaw Wraps

Crisping up wraps takes just a few minutes but really improves the flavor. Try it with store-bought wraps, too.

2 large (about 11 inches in diameter) white, whole wheat, or flavored wraps

½ pound sliced smoked or regular turkey breast

¼ pound thinly sliced Muenster cheese

6 thin slices tomato (optional)

2 tablespoons bottled barbecue sauce

⅔ cup Easy or Easier Coleslaw (page 119) or store-bought creamy coleslaw

Vegetable oil

1. Lay the wraps out flat. Picture a square in the center of each wrap and cover it with an even layer of turkey, then cheese. Lay the tomato slices, if using, over the cheese. Stir the barbecue sauce into the coleslaw and spread evenly over the other ingredients. Fold the bottom of the wrap over the filling ingredients, then fold both sides over the filling. Starting at the bottom, roll the wrap up into a compact roll.

2. Lightly coat the bottom of a heavy, large skillet with oil. Heat over medium-low heat. Set the wraps into the skillet, flap-side down. Cook until lightly browned and crispy, about 4 minutes. Flip and repeat. Whether serving cold or warm, cut each wrap in half on the bias.

SERVES 4 KIDS OR 2 ADULTS

French Toast for Breakfast (or Dinner) with Blueberry Syrup

Here's a good, grown-up version of French toast that will be a hit with kids, too. If you like things sweeter, up the sugar in the egg batter and/or blueberry syrup and go heavy on the confectioners' sugar when serving.

FOR THE BLUEBERRY SYRUP

One 12-ounce bag frozen blueberries
⅔ cup confectioners' sugar
Large pinch of ground cinnamon

FOR THE FRENCH TOAST

5 large eggs
¼ cup milk
2 tablespoons granulated sugar
1 teaspoon pure vanilla extract
Pinch of salt
Six ½-inch-thick slices egg bread, such as challah or brioche, or 4 thick slices raisin bread or soft white bread
Vegetable oil cooking spray or unsalted butter
Confectioners' sugar

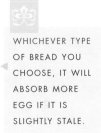

WHICHEVER TYPE OF BREAD YOU CHOOSE, IT WILL ABSORB MORE EGG IF IT IS SLIGHTLY STALE.

1. Make the syrup: Toss the frozen blueberries with the confectioners' sugar in a heavy, medium saucepan. Place over low heat and cook, stirring, until the liquid given off by the blueberries starts to simmer. Stir in the cinnamon, remove from the heat, and cover to keep warm. (The syrup can be made up to a few days in advance. Refrigerate in the pan and rewarm over low heat before serving.)

2. Heat a griddle over medium-low heat until a few drops of water flicked onto the surface take a full 3 seconds to evaporate. If the water evaporates more quickly, reduce the heat; if it takes longer, increase the heat. (Alternatively, heat an electric griddle to 325°F.) Beat the eggs, milk, granulated sugar, vanilla, and salt

CONTINUED

together in a 13 x 9-inch baking dish (or any container large enough to hold the bread comfortably) until thoroughly blended. Add the bread to the dish and let soak 1 minute. Flip and repeat. Most if not all of the egg mixture will be absorbed.

3. Lightly grease the griddle with cooking spray or butter. Lift the slices one at a time and set them on the griddle. Cook until the underside is a deep golden brown, about 4 minutes. Flip the slices and cook until the second side is golden brown, about 3 minutes. Serve on warm plates. Spoon a little blueberry syrup over each serving and sprinkle with confectioners' sugar.

SERVES 2 (THE RECIPE CAN BE EASILY DOUBLED.)

Buttermilk-Soaked Fried Chicken

The simplest way to get pieces of chicken down to the right size for frying is to buy a chicken already cut into eighths, available in all supermarkets.

1 chicken (about 3 ½ pounds), cut into eighths
1 ½ cups buttermilk
1 tablespoon salt
½ teaspoon cayenne pepper
All-purpose flour
Vegetable shortening or vegetable oil as needed (about 1 ½ cups)

1. Trim any overhanging fat from the chicken pieces. If there are pieces of the backbone attached to the thigh and breast pieces, cut them off with kitchen shears. Cut off the wing tips. (Save the backbones, wing tips, and giblets for Chicken Broth, page 37.) Cut each breast in half crosswise with a sharp, heavy knife.

2. Stir the buttermilk, salt, and cayenne pepper together in a large bowl. Add the chicken pieces and toss gently to coat with seasoned buttermilk. Cover and refrigerate at least 4 hours or up to overnight.

3. When ready to fry, spread the flour out in a generous layer on a baking sheet. Have ready a wire cooling rack set over a baking sheet. Lift each piece of chicken from the buttermilk, holding it over the bowl and wiping off all but a light layer of buttermilk. Lay as many of the chicken pieces in the flour as fit without touching. Clean and dry your hands. Shake the baking sheet to turn and evenly coat the chicken pieces, then turn them by hand to make sure they are lightly but evenly coated. Lift the chicken, tap off any excess flour, and set, skin-side up, on the rack. Repeat with the remaining chicken.

4. Melt enough shortening in (or pour enough oil into) a wide deep skillet to fill 1 inch. (A 10-inch cast-iron skillet will hold half a chicken.) Heat over medium heat to 325°F. If you don't have a deep-frying thermometer, dip the handle of a wooden spoon in the oil. When it is hot enough, the handle will send out a steady, lively stream of tiny bubbles. Lay as many pieces of coated chicken, skin-side down, into the pan as will fit comfortably, leaving a little space between each. Don't move the chicken until it begins to brown, or the delicate

CONTINUED

coating will stick to the pan. Adjust the heat so there is a steady, not riotous, sizzling. If there is any spattering or if the chicken starts to brown even slightly before 4 minutes, the heat is definitely too high. Cook until the underside is a deep golden brown, about 12 minutes. Flip and cook the second side. If the heat was regulated properly, the chicken should be fully cooked. Check by inserting the tip of an instant-reading thermometer into the thickest part of each chicken piece closest to the bone. The temperature should be 165°F or above. Alternatively, poke the tip of a paring knife into the thickest part of each piece right down to the bone. Wait a second or two; the juices that run out must be clear, not pink, in order for the chicken to be safe to eat. If the chicken browns before it is fully cooked, simply finish cooking the chicken, testing as above, on a baking sheet in a 375°F oven.

SERVES 4

Note: The chicken can be served warm or at room temperature. If you'd like to serve the chicken warm, preheat the oven to 200°F. Fry the drumsticks and thighs first, drain them, and keep them warm on a baking sheet in the oven while frying the breast and wing pieces.

Slow Cooker Pot Roast

Combine with the Old-School Buttered Noodles on page 198 to round out this classic dish. This makes a thin gravy, but it can be thickened lightly with cornstarch if you prefer (see Note on page 186).

One 3½- to 4-pound beef pot roast (rump or bottom round)
Vegetable oil
3 cups canned beef broth
2 tablespoons tomato paste
2 tablespoons Dijon mustard
One 1-pound bag baby carrots
One 10-ounce package small cremini mushrooms
1 large yellow onion, cut into ½-inch slices
2 bay leaves
Salt and freshly ground black pepper (optional)

1. Pat the beef dry on all sides with paper towels. Pour enough vegetable oil into a large skillet to film the bottom and heat over medium-high heat until rippling. Add the beef and cook, turning with large tongs or two forks, until well browned on all sides, about 12 minutes.

2. Meanwhile, whisk the broth, tomato paste, and mustard together in the cooker. Put the beef in the cooker and scatter the vegetables over and around the beef, distributing them more or less evenly. Add the bay leaves. Set the cooker to High/8 hours.

3. Toward the end of cooking, taste the cooking broth and season with salt and pepper if necessary.

4. Remove the beef to a carving board. With a slotted spoon, scoop the vegetables around the border of a large platter or into a serving bowl. Carve the beef against the grain into ¼-inch slices. Arrange the slices overlapping down the center of the platter or onto individual plates. Discard the bay leaves and ladle some of

CONTINUED

the cooking liquid into a gravy boat. (Any remaining liquid can be frozen and used in place of canned broth for the next slow-cooked pot roast.) Serve hot.

SERVES 8

Note: To thicken gravy, ladle 2 cups or so of the cooking liquid into a small saucepan. Bring to a simmer over low heat. Stir 2 tablespoons cornstarch and ¼ cup water together in a small bowl until smooth. Stir into the saucepan and cook, stirring, until the gravy is thickened.

Stovetop-Barbecued Pork Chops

The next time your barbecue is rained out or you crave the taste of summer in the dead of winter, think of these chops. The ingredients—with the exception of the pork chops—are most likely in your fridge and pantry.

Four 10-ounce loin pork chops, each about ¾ inch thick

Salt and freshly ground black pepper

⅓ cup tomato purée

¼ cup Chicken Broth (page 37), store-bought chicken broth, or water

1 tablespoon white vinegar

1 tablespoon light or dark brown sugar

2 teaspoons Worcestershire sauce

½ teaspoon garlic powder

1 tablespoon vegetable oil

Hot red pepper sauce (optional)

◄◄ CHOOSE CHOPS WITH A COMPACT SHAPE SO ALL FOUR CHOPS FIT IN THE SKILLET AT THE SAME TIME IN A SINGLE LAYER.

1. Pat the chops dry with paper towels. Season both sides generously with salt and pepper. Whisk the purée, broth, vinegar, sugar, Worcestershire sauce, and garlic powder together in a small bowl until blended.

2. Choose a heavy pan in which the chops will fit snugly in a single layer (about 12 inches wide). Heat the oil in the pan over medium-high heat. Add the chops and cook until the underside is golden brown, about 5 minutes. If the fat begins to spatter, lower the heat slightly. Flip the chops and cook until the underside is light golden brown, about 4 minutes.

3. Pour the purée mixture into the pan and bring to a boil. Adjust the heat so the liquid is boiling gently. Cook until the sauce is thickened enough to glaze the chops. Turn the chops in the sauce and transfer them to serving plates or a platter. Taste the sauce, adding hot red pepper sauce and salt and/or pepper, if you like. Spoon the sauce over the chops and serve hot.

SERVES 4

Meat Loaf

Here we are—a juicy, simple meat loaf packed with flavor and made with ingredients most likely on hand (except for the ground beef and scallions). The sauce from the Stuffed Cabbage on page 44 makes a nice accompaniment.

The sauce from the Stuffed Cabbage on page 44 makes a nice accompaniment.

PACKAGES OF MEAT LOAF MIX, USUALLY A BLEND OF PORK, VEAL, AND BEEF, ARE AVAILABLE IN MANY SUPERMARKETS. IF YOU LIKE, SUBSTITUTE AN EQUAL AMOUNT OF THIS MIX FOR THE BEEF LISTED IN THE INGREDIENTS.

▶ ▶ 2 pounds ground chuck (85% lean)

¾ cup plain bread crumbs

4 scallions, trimmed and very thinly sliced

1 medium carrot, peeled, trimmed, and coarsely grated

2 large eggs

3 tablespoons Worcestershire sauce

3 tablespoons mustard

2 tablespoons tomato paste

1 teaspoon crumbled dried thyme

1 teaspoon salt

¼ teaspoon freshly ground black pepper

1. Preheat the oven to 375°F.

2. Crumble the ground beef into a large mixing bowl. Scatter the bread crumbs, scallions, and carrot over the beef. In a separate bowl, beat the eggs, Worcestershire sauce, mustard, tomato paste, thyme, salt, and pepper. Pour over the beef and mix thoroughly with your hands until all the ingredients are evenly distributed through the beef.

3. Transfer the meat loaf to a baking sheet. With wet hands, shape into a smooth, even 9 x 5 x 2-inch loaf. Bake until no trace of pink remains near the center, about 50 minutes. (An instant-reading thermometer inserted into the center of the loaf will register 160°F.) Remove and let stand 5 minutes. Serve hot, cut into 1-inch slices.

SERVES 6

Better-Than-Packaged Breading

Part of Lynette's arsenal of kid-friendly dinner staples, this homemade version of a supermarket classic contains only quality ingredients of your choosing—herbs, seasonings, and bread crumbs. Mixed with a small amount of vegetable oil, it is ready to coat all manner of oven-baked foods, chicken parts, chops, and fish fillets.

1 ½ cups plain bread crumbs
2 tablespoons salt
2 tablespoons dried thyme
1 tablespoon dried oregano
1 tablespoon dried sage
1 tablespoon paprika
1 ½ teaspoons freshly ground black pepper

Mix all the ingredients together in a bowl until well blended. Store in an airtight container in a cool, dark place for up to 2 months.

MAKES 1 ½ CUPS MIX

TO SERVE 4:

Rub ½ cup crumb-oil mixture together with 1 teaspoon vegetable oil until the crumbs are the texture of wet sand. Spread the crumbs out on a plate and pat gently into both sides of the meat or fish.

PORK CHOPS:

Preheat the oven to 425°F. Use the crumb-oil mixture to coat both sides of four 8- to 9-ounce, 1-inch-thick pork chops. Arrange the chops on a nonstick baking sheet (or a lightly oiled baking sheet). Bake until no trace of pink remains near the bone and the coating is golden brown, about 20 minutes.

CHICKEN BREASTS:

Preheat the oven to 450°F. Use the crumb mixture to coat both sides of four 7-ounce, 1 ¼-inch-thick boneless, skinless chicken breasts. Arrange the chicken on a nonstick baking sheet (or a lightly oiled baking sheet). Bake until no trace of pink remains at the center of the thickest part and the coating is golden brown, about 15 minutes.

FISH FILLETS:

Preheat the oven to 475°F. Use the crumb-oil mixture to coat both sides of four 8-ounce, 1 ¼-inch-thick firm white fish fillets (such as catfish, flounder, or cod). Arrange the fillets on a nonstick baking sheet (or a lightly oiled baking sheet). Bake until opaque throughout and the coating is golden brown, about 12 minutes.

Mary Todd Lincoln

Most well known for sitting next to her husband in Ford's Theater when he was shot in the head by John Wilkes Booth, Mary Todd Lincoln led an even more heartbreaking and tragic life than most members of the public were aware. Less than ten years after her husband's death, she would be sent to an insane asylum—having lost everything near and dear to her.

Mary Todd Lincoln's life did not begin on a sad note. Born in 1818 to a wealthy Kentucky family, Mary moved in with her sister in Springfield, Illinois, when she reached adulthood, and soon met and married the love of her life, then–law student Abraham Lincoln. The man she married, of course, was elected president during a particularly contentious time for the United States. To many people, he became perhaps the greatest American president in history.

Life in the White House, however, was far from perfect. Having lost one of their children before coming to Washington, the couple suffered their greatest loss while in the White House—the death of Mary's favorite son, Willie, in 1862. Before her son's death, Mary was the typical First Lady, albeit more on the extravagant side than most—spending large amounts of money on clothing and entertainment. After Willie's death, she stopped entertaining and was accused of shirking her responsibilities as First Lady. To be fair, the public did not exactly have a great love affair with Mrs. Lincoln even before the tragedy. Her leaning toward opulence, Southern heritage (therefore bringing into question her loyalties during the Civil War), and carefree style did not sit well with Washington insiders and many Americans in general.

Although their temperaments were radically different, the marriage of Mary and Abraham Lincoln was apparently a strong one. This was especially important since Abraham rather notoriously suffered melancholia—a quaint term for what we now call depression—and was therefore prone to bouts of severe misery and hopelessness.

After the assassination, Mary Todd Lincoln was so shaken that she was unable to leave the White House for weeks. (Much like our own Bree Van De Kamp, her world crumbled when her husband died.) When she finally did leave Washington for Chicago, she was a different woman. Obsessed with poverty and unable to access her husband's money at the time—since it was legally tied up—Mary began to lose her grip on reality and quickly descended from a tortured soul into a woman declared insane.

To add the ultimate insult to injury, Mary was institutionalized based upon the testimony of her only surviving child, Robert Todd Lincoln (who has the curious distinction of being present during the assassination of or assassination attempt on three different U.S. presidents). She died seven years later. One can assume a broken heart was one of many causes.

Glazed Brussels Sprouts

L ike mothers everywhere, Lynette knows that brussels sprouts are a tough sell when it comes to kids. Here, a light orange-honey glaze may make them a bit more appealing to kids and borderline irresistible to adults.

Salt
Two 1-pint containers large brussels sprouts (about 1 ½ pounds)
1 tablespoon vegetable oil
1 tablespoon butter
1 medium yellow onion, cut into ¼-inch dice (about 1 cup)
3 tablespoons orange juice
1 tablespoon honey
Freshly ground black pepper

1. Bring a large saucepan of salted water to a boil.

2. Meanwhile, trim the stems flush with the bottom of each sprout. Cut the sprouts in half through the core and slip the sprouts into the boiling water. Cook for 5 minutes after the water returns to the boil. Drain thoroughly.

3. Heat the vegetable oil and butter in a large skillet until the butter is foaming. Add the onion and cook, stirring occasionally, until light brown, about 8 minutes. Stir in the drained brussels sprouts and cook, stirring occasionally, until very tender and browned, about 14 minutes. Make sure to stir gently but thoroughly so none of the sprouts stick or burn.

4. Stir the orange juice and honey together in a small bowl until the honey is dissolved. Increase the heat to high and pour the honey mixture into the pan. Bring to a boil and cook, stirring constantly, until the liquid is evaporated and the sprouts are coated with a shiny glaze. Remove the pan from the heat and season to taste with salt and pepper. Serve immediately. The sprouts can be fully cooked up to 2 hours before serving and reheated in a baking dish in a 375°F oven for 20 minutes.

SERVES 4

Potato Casserole

1 cup Chicken Broth (page 37) or store-bought chicken broth

1 cup light cream

2 large russet (Idaho) potatoes (about 1 ½ pounds)

1 medium leek, cleaned (see page 5) and cut into ¼-inch slices

Salt and freshly ground black pepper

¼ cup plain dry bread crumbs

1 cup grated jack or Swiss cheese (about 3 ounces)

1. Place a rack in the top position and preheat the oven to 375°F. Pour the broth and cream into a 9 x 11-inch or oval 12-inch baking dish.

2. Peel the potatoes and wash them. Cut them into ½-inch dice, adding them to the baking dish. Scatter the leek over the potatoes, season lightly to taste with salt and pepper, and stir well. Bake until the potatoes are softened but still firm at the center, about 25 minutes.

3. Scatter the bread crumbs over the casserole and stir well. Taste and add salt and pepper, if you like. Top with an even layer of cheese. Bake until most of the liquid is absorbed, the potatoes are tender, and the top of the casserole is a rich golden brown, about 15 minutes. Let stand 5 minutes before serving.

SERVES 6

eggs	tomatoes
Fish sticks	fun-shaped pasta
Fruit roll-ups	Lunch meat
Chicken nuggets	apples
Easy fries	bananas
Hot dogs	Diet soda
white hot dog buns	Red Bull
	Coffee
Wonder bread	Espresso
Peanut butter and jelly	Chocolate-covered espresso beans
Juice boxes	Lunchables
baby cereal	chips
diapers (size 3)	brown Lunch Bags
Toilet paper max pack	frozen food
Pepto-Bismol	
Hamburger meat	
Tortillas	
Rolaids	
lettuce	

Broccoli or Cauliflower
with Seasoned Bread Crumbs

You can make this side dish with a mixture of both vegetables if there are odds and ends of each in the vegetable drawer. It's also a good thing to keep in mind if your supermarket sells small containers of raw broccoli and cauliflower florets.

Salt

6 cups broccoli florets, no bigger than 2 inches across
    (from about 4 medium stalks of broccoli) or 4 cups cauliflower florets,
    no bigger than 2 ½ inches across (from 1 large head)

Vegetable oil

⅓ cup Better-Than-Packaged Breading (page 190)

2 tablespoons finely grated Parmesan cheese

2 tablespoons melted butter or vegetable oil

1. Bring a large saucepan of salted water to a boil. Boil the florets until the thickest part of the stem is barely tender but still quite firm, about 4 minutes after the water returns to a boil for broccoli and 5 minutes for cauliflower. Drain, rinse briefly under cold water, and drain thoroughly. Spread out on a double thickness of paper towel to drain and cool completely.

2. Put a rack in the center position and preheat the oven to 400°F. Generously oil a baking sheet.

3. Mix the breading, cheese, and melted butter together in a large bowl. Toss half the florets in the breading. Press the crumbs lightly onto the florets. The breading will not completely coat the florets nor will it coat them evenly; that is fine. Set the florets on the prepared sheet. Repeat with the remaining florets.

4. Bake until the coating is golden brown and the florets are tender, about 12 minutes. Serve hot, warm, or at room temperature.

SERVES 4

Old-School Buttered Noodles

4 cups curly wide egg noodles
2 tablespoons unsalted butter, at room temperature
2 tablespoons chopped fresh parsley or dill
Salt and freshly ground black pepper

1. Cook the noodles in a medium saucepan of salted water until al dente, 4 to 5 minutes. (When you bite into one, there should be a very thin ribbon of white at the center.) While the noodles are cooking, put the butter and parsley or dill in a small bowl.

2. Spoon ¼ cup of the cooking water into the bowl with the butter. Drain the noodles thoroughly, bouncing them gently in the colander to remove as much water as possible. Return the noodles to the pan, place over medium heat, and add the butter-water mixture. Cook, stirring gently, until the water is evaporated and the noodles are glossy. Remove from the heat and season to taste with salt and pepper.

SERVES 4

Match the Desperate Housewife with Her Favorite Movie:

1. *The Remains of the Day*
2. *When Harry Met Sally*
3. *9 ½ Weeks*
4. *Working Girl*
5. *Breakfast at Tiffany's*

A. Susan Mayer
B. Edie Britt
C. Bree Van De Kamp
D. Gabrielle Solis
E. Lynette Scavo

Answers:

1 C. **Bree.** She loves anything that prizes decorum above all else. Even love.

2 A. **Susan.** An impossible romantic, Susan loves the roller-coaster ride of romance in the Billy Crystal/Meg Ryan film.

3 B. **Edie.** The movie has sex, bondage, and obsession. No further comment.

4 E. **Lynette** was so in awe of the villainous boss played by Sigourney Weaver, she was inspired to seek out an MBA.

5 D. **Gabrielle** is torn between *Breakfast at Tiffany's* and *Pretty Woman* as her all-time favorite fantasies, but goes with *Breakfast* for the wardrobe (and Audrey Hepburn, of course).

Coffee Frappe

Lynette has many close friends on Wisteria Lane, but few know the truth about her true *best* friend—caffeine. From the morning cup of coffee at home to jump-start her day getting the kids ready for school, to the midday diet cola to liven up her presentations, to the espresso she shares with Tom after dinner, Lynette's dark secret is none other than caffeine addiction. After trying this frappe, you might find yourself vying for Lynette's best friend's attention.

3 coffee ice cubes (see Box below)
½ cup whole milk
¼ cup reduced-fat evaporated milk
1 packet artificial sweetener or 1 tablespoon superfine sugar

Combine all the ingredients in a blender and blend at high speed until smooth. Pour into a tall chilled glass.

SERVES 1

Next time there is part of a pot of coffee left over, think of this refreshing pick-me-up. Pour the coffee into ice cube trays and, once frozen, transfer the cubes to a sealable bag and keep in the freezer. Take this recipe from naughty to light by substituting soy milk or skim milk for the whole milk and evaporated milk. The texture will be icy rather than smooth and creamy, but the taste is still delicious.

Lynette on Cake Mix

When I went to business school, I learned a dirty little secret about "instant" cake mix—the kind that fills the shelves at your local supermarket. Way back in the 1960s, the major food companies came up with instant mix that required only one additional ingredient to prepare a chocolate cake: that good old staple of even the most basic kitchen—water. However, they found in research testing that the average housewife did not feel like she was an integral part of the baking process with this "too simple" recipe, so they rejiggered the formula to include more. The new version of the cake mix now required eggs, milk, and other ingredients. Was this supposed to make women feel as if they were doing their wifely duties?

I have four children. Do you know how much time I spend baking cakes? Between birthdays, holidays, and the endless parade of parties that kids seem to require, I can't even count anymore. Do you know how much happier I'd be if I only had to add water and put it in the oven? Ladies, if you want to feel good about making a cake, make it from scratch! Otherwise, let the rest of us be lazy (or, as I prefer to say, "more time efficient").

Babysitting Cookies

Bree never fails to whip up a batch of these when Lynette presses her into babysitting duty. Lynette made them part of her repertoire when she saw how even her kids manage to behave when a plate of these looms as a reward.

1 ½ cups all-purpose flour
¾ teaspoon baking powder
8 tablespoons (1 stick) unsalted butter
¾ cup sugar, plus more for the tops of the cookies
1 egg
1 teaspoon pure vanilla extract
¾ cup smooth or chunky peanut butter
About ½ cup chocolate chips

1. Set a rack in the center position and preheat the oven to 350°F. Lightly grease a cookie sheet or line with parchment paper.

2. Stir the flour and baking powder together in a small bowl and set aside. Beat the butter and ¾ cup sugar together in a medium bowl with a handheld mixer at high speed until smooth. Beat in the egg and vanilla. Add the peanut butter and beat until smooth. Stir in the dry ingredients just until no streaks of white remain.

3. Using 2 tablespoons of the batter, form a ball and place it on the prepared baking sheet. Press with the bottom of a glass to form a 2 ½-inch circle. Repeat with the remaining dough, using two baking sheets if necessary. Make smiley faces ☺ using 1 chip for each eye and 4 chips for the smile, pressing the chips, point-side down, into the dough. Sprinkle sugar liberally over the tops. Bake until the edges are lightly browned, about 20 minutes. Remove and cool completely before serving. The cookies can be stored in an airtight container for up to 4 days.

MAKES 20 COOKIES

Mango Martinis

12 ounces vodka

4 ounces Cointreau

4 ounces mango juice (not nectar), or more to taste

Pineapple wedges for garnish

Stir everything except the pineapple wedges together and chill. You'll have to stir again before pouring into the shaker because the mango juice will settle to the bottom. Pour over lots of ice and shake vigorously. Pour into chilled martini glasses. A wedge of fresh pineapple makes a nice garnish.

MAKES 4 GOOD-SIZE OR 6 SMALLER DRINKS

Deviled Crab Dip

There are all kinds of crabmeat out there. Use a less pricey type, like backfin or plain lump meat from blue claw crabs—any type of crabmeat that will keep its shape will do.

½ cup cream cheese, softened
½ cup mayonnaise
1 large celery stalk, trimmed and finely chopped (about ½ cup)
2 tablespoons Dijon or spicy mustard
One 8-ounce container backfin or lump crabmeat, drained
Paprika

Crackers, Perfect Crostini (page 222), or pita chips (page 85) for dipping

Beat the cream cheese, mayonnaise, celery, and mustard together in a mixing bowl until thoroughly blended. Pick over the crabmeat to remove pieces of shell and cartilage, if any. Stir into the dip. Sprinkle with paprika before serving. The dip can be served at room temperature, chilled (for up to a day), or warm. To warm, scrape the dip into a heatproof 4-cup dish. Bake at 300°F until warmed through, about 15 minutes. Serve with crackers or other dippers.

MAKES 2 ½ CUPS

Classic Bistro-Style Mussels in White Wine

Cultivated mussels are widely available, require very little prep, and cook in a flash. If you like, you can make the onion-wine mixture up to two days in advance. Serve this with a thin loaf of crusty bread torn into rough pieces or turn it into a main course for six by serving it over a pound of spaghetti, boiled until al dente and drained.

One 2-pound bag or 2 pounds loose mussels, preferably cultivated
2 tablespoons olive oil
1 medium yellow onion, thinly sliced
1 cup dry white wine
¼ cup heavy cream (optional)
Coarsely ground black pepper
2 tablespoons finely chopped fresh Italian parsley or chives

1. Rinse the mussels under plenty of cold water. Check the mussels and scrape off any matter stuck to the shells. If necessary (most likely not with cultivated mussels), pull off the "beards," the wiry growth that sticks out of the flat side of the shell. Discard any mussels that open again after pressing the shells closed.

2. Heat the oil in a wide, deep pan or flameproof casserole over medium heat. Add the onion and cook, stirring, until wilted but not browned, about 4 minutes. Add the white wine, bring to a boil, and cook until reduced by about half. Pour in the cream, if using, season to taste with pepper, and add the mussels. Raise the heat to high, cover the pot, and cook until all the mussels are open, about 4 minutes. Remove from the heat, stir in the herb of choice, and ladle the mussels and liquid into warm shallow serving bowls. Set an additional bowl or two on the table for shells.

SERVES 4 AS A FIRST COURSE

Do-Ahead Mushroom Soufflé

Soufflés have gotten a needlessly bad rap over the past decade. They are simple to make and even easier to serve to guests. Even better, just about any kind of soufflé batter can be scooped into its dish and refrigerated, then popped right from the fridge into the oven. (See the Note on page 211 if you'd like to make and bake the soufflé without refrigerating it.)

Chopping the mushrooms very, very fine helps them stay suspended in the soufflé instead of sinking to the bottom.

FOR THE THICK BÉCHAMEL

5 tablespoons unsalted butter

5 tablespoons all-purpose flour

2 ½ cups hot milk

1 teaspoon salt

¼ teaspoon freshly ground black pepper

FOR THE SOUFFLÉ

Softened unsalted butter

¼ cup finely grated Parmesan or Asiago cheese

One 10-ounce package white or cremini mushrooms, wiped clean, trimmed, and quartered

1 tablespoon vegetable oil

Salt

4 eggs, separated

1 cup shredded Gruyère or Swiss cheese

2 teaspoons Dijon mustard

⅛ teaspoon grated nutmeg

1. Make the Béchamel Sauce according to the recipe on page 114. Scrape the sauce into a large mixing bowl and let cool to warm, whisking occasionally so the sauce doesn't form a skin on top.

2. Generously butter an 8-cup soufflé dish. (Don't miss the corners.) Sprinkle the grated Parmesan over the bottom, then roll and tap the

CONTINUED

SOUFFLÉ DISHES COME IN ALL SIZES AND SHAPES. THIS RECIPE CALLS FOR AN 8-CUP SOUFFLÉ DISH. SOME DISHES MARKED "6-CUP" WILL HOLD 6 CUPS OF LIQUID WHEN FILLED TO THE RIM; OTHERS WILL HOLD 6 CUPS WHEN FILLED TO THE BOTTOM OF THE LIP THAT RUNS AROUND THE EDGE OF MOST DISHES. THIS AMOUNT OF BATTER WILL WORK BEST IN A FULL 8-CUP DISH.

dish to cover the entire bottom and sides evenly with cheese. Set the prepared dish and the remaining Parmesan aside.

3. Working in 3 batches, chop the mushrooms in a food processor using quick on/off pulses until very finely chopped. Heat the oil in a large skillet over medium heat until rippling. Add the mushrooms and season them lightly with salt. The mushrooms will give off a lot of liquid. Continue cooking and stirring until the liquid is evaporated and the mushrooms are dry and start to stick to the pan, about 10 minutes. Remove from the heat.

4. When the béchamel is body temperature, beat in the egg yolks one at a time. Stir in the shredded Gruyère, the remaining Parmesan, and the mustard and nutmeg. Fold in the mushrooms.

5. In a separate mixing bowl, beat the egg whites with a handheld mixer at high speed (or by hand with a wire whisk) just until they hold soft peaks when the beaters are lifted from them. Don't overbeat or the soufflé won't rise as dramatically. Take a big spoonful of the egg whites and stir it gently into the mushroom mixture. Scrape the remaining whites on top of the mushroom mixture and fold them in with a rubber spatula, lifting the batter from the bottom of the bowl up and over the whites. Fold until just a streak or two of egg whites remains. Scrape the soufflé into the prepared dish. Refrigerate with a piece of plastic wrap pressed lightly to the surface for up to 1 day.

6. Set a baking sheet on a center rack and preheat the oven to 375°F. Set the dish on the baking sheet. Bake until the top is deep golden brown and the center wiggles slightly when the pan is moved very gently back and forth, about 45 minutes.

7. Remove the baking sheet from the oven. Wait 1 minute, then serve, including some of the crispy outer portion and creamy center with each serving.

SERVES 4 AS A MAIN COURSE OR 6 TO 8 AS A FIRST COURSE

TO SERVE THE SOUFFLÉ WITHOUT REFRIGERATING:

Prepare as above. After making the béchamel, set the baking sheet on a center rack and preheat the oven to 400°F. As soon as the beaten egg whites are folded into the batter, set the dish on the baking sheet and bake until risen and deep golden brown, about 35 minutes. Serve as above.

Broiled-Baked Salmon Fillets with Mustard Bread Crumbs

By combining the top browning heat from a broiler with the heat the broiler creates in the oven, these salmon fillets emerge with a crunchy top coat of crumbs and a medium-rare interior. If you like your salmon more well done, turn off the broiler and leave the fillets in the oven a few minutes longer.

1 cup coarse dry bread crumbs (see Note on page 213)
3 tablespoons grainy mustard
1 tablespoon fresh lemon juice
1 tablespoon vegetable oil
1 tablespoon light brown sugar
1 teaspoon salt
Several grinds of black pepper
4 salmon fillets, skins left on, each 7 to 8 ounces and as close to
    1 ¼ inches thick as possible

1. Set a rack about 8 inches from the broiler and preheat the broiler to low.

2. Spread the bread crumbs out in an even layer on a plate. Beat the mustard, lemon juice, oil, brown sugar, salt, and pepper together in a medium bowl. Dip one fillet in the mustard mixture to coat all but the skin side evenly and generously. Then roll it in the bread crumbs to completely cover all but the skin side, patting the crumbs gently to help them stick. Place the fillet, skin-side down, on an aluminum foil–lined baking sheet. Repeat with the remaining fillets. The fillets can be seasoned and coated up to 2 hours in advance. Cover the baking sheet with plastic wrap and refrigerate. If necessary, uncover the salmon and let stand at room temperature while the broiler is heating.

3. Bake/broil until the coating is a rich golden brown and the fillets are cooked to medium, about 8 minutes. Check the fillets once or twice to make sure the bread crumb coating is not browning too quickly. If so, move the fillets farther from the broiler or turn off the broiler for a minute or so. Serve immediately.

IF YOU'D LIKE TO SERVE THE FILLETS WITHOUT SKIN, SIMPLY SLIP A METAL SPATULA BETWEEN THE SKIN AND THE FILLET AFTER BAKING AND LIFT THE FILLET ONTO THE PLATE, LEAVING THE SKIN BEHIND.

◂◂

SERVES 4

Note: Panko are Japanese-style bread crumbs made from white bread. They are coarse in texture, very dry, and perfect for this recipe. If you cannot find them in an Asian or specialty store or online (see Sources, page 266), make your own: Cut the crust from day-old bread. (The bread should feel stale but not be completely dry or the crumbs will be too fine.) Cut the bread into 1-inch cubes and put them in a food processor. With quick on/off pulses, process the bread to form coarse crumbs. Spread out the crumbs on a baking sheet and let stand at room temperature until dry, 1 to 2 days, depending on the humidity. If you have an oven with a gas pilot light, you can dry the crumbs in the oven while it is off.

Roasted Asparagus with Parmesan Cheese

Sprinkling cheese over the asparagus will cause the spears to stick together. Break the row of asparagus apart into little "rafts." Center the rafts on dinner plates and use them to float whatever entrée you like. The effect works beautifully with the Broiled-Baked Salmon Fillets with Mustard Bread Crumbs on page 212.

1 pound medium asparagus (stalks between ¼ and ½ inch thick)
1 tablespoon butter, melted
Salt
Freshly ground black pepper
¼ cup coarsely shredded Parmesan cheese

1. To trim the tough ends from the asparagus, grasp each stalk of asparagus firmly at its tip. Bend the stalk end and the tough end will snap off, leaving the more tender part of the stalk. Peel the stalks from the base right up to the tip. The asparagus can be prepared up to a day in advance. Wrap the stalks in paper towels and store the bundle in a plastic bag in the vegetable drawer of your refrigerator.

2. When ready to serve, preheat the oven to 450°F. Spread the asparagus out on a baking sheet. Drizzle the butter over them, then rub until the asparagus are coated evenly. Sprinkle the asparagus with salt and pepper. Use the flat end of a metal spatula to nudge the asparagus together so there is no space between the stalks. Roast until the asparagus are tender, about 10 minutes. The asparagus can be prepared to this point up to 2 hours in advance. Let stand at room temperature.

3. Sprinkle the cheese evenly over the stalks, leaving the tips bare. Return to the oven until the cheese is melted, about 2 minutes for freshly roasted asparagus or up to 4 minutes for asparagus that has been standing. Serve immediately, breaking the long row into 4 equal pieces or into individual stalks, as you like.

SERVES 4

Look-Ma-No-Hands Mushrooms

A boon to busy mothers-and-others who need a quick side dish, this is delicious hot from the oven or at room temperature.

2 tablespoons olive oil

2 teaspoons lemon juice or white wine vinegar

1 teaspoon salt

½ teaspoon ground cumin

Two 10-ounce packages fresh cremini or white mushrooms, wiped clean with a damp paper towel

1. Preheat the oven to 450°F.

2. Stir the oil, lemon juice, salt, and cumin together in a 13 x 11-inch baking dish. Trim the stem ends from the mushrooms and cut the mushrooms into quarters. Toss them in the seasoning mix in the baking dish to coat as evenly as possible. Spread the mushrooms out in an even layer. Roast, stirring once about halfway through, until browned and tender, 20 minutes. Serve hot or cold.

SERVES 4

Irresistible Brownies

These rich brownies walk a fine line between fudgy and cakey and embody the best of both types. They freeze beautifully, too.

12 ounces good-quality semisweet or bittersweet chocolate,
   broken or cut into 1-inch pieces

1 cup sugar

1 ½ sticks (12 tablespoons) unsalted butter, plus more for the baking pan

1 cup all-purpose flour, plus more for the baking pan

2 teaspoons baking powder

¼ teaspoon salt

4 large eggs

1 tablespoon pure vanilla extract

1 ½ cups chopped walnuts or pecans (optional)

1. Melt the chocolate, sugar, and butter in the top of a double boiler over barely simmering water (or in a heatproof bowl set over a pot of barely simmering water). Stir occasionally until the chocolate is melted and the mixture is smooth, about 10 minutes. Make sure the water stays at a bare simmer; if it gets too hot, the chocolate will separate. Cool to room temperature.

2. Heat the oven to 350°F. Lightly butter and flour a 13 x 9-inch baking pan.

3. Stir the flour, baking powder, and salt together in a bowl and set aside. Beat the cooled chocolate mixture with a handheld mixer at medium speed until shiny. Add the eggs one at a time, beating very well after each. Beat in the vanilla. Stir in the dry ingredients just until no streaks of white remain. Fold in the nuts, if using. Pour the batter into the prepared pan and smooth into an even layer.

4. Bake until the edges are crisp and begin to pull away from the pan and the top is set, about 18 minutes. (The center of the brownies will still be slightly soft to the touch and a toothpick or cake tester inserted in the center will not come out clean.) Let cool completely.

5. Cut the brownies into 2 x 3-inch bars. This is easier if the brownies are chilled in the pan for 10 to 20 minutes first. The brownies may be made up to 2 days in advance and refrigerated, covered. Bring to room temperature before serving. The brownies may also be frozen, well wrapped in aluminum foil.

MAKES SIXTEEN 3 X 2-INCH BROWNIES

Edie

The "virtue-deprived" flirt

of Wisteria Lane is none other than Susan's worst nightmare and everyone's favorite real estate agent, Edie Britt. Edie has a rather unhealthy obsession with food. In fact, she thinks that all food in general is erotic . . . as well as at her mercy.

Edie truly believes the axiom "The way to a man's heart is through his stomach." The truth is that usually she doesn't actually care about the man's heart, only the rippling muscles that surround it. So Edie's menu is quite different from the other women's on Wisteria Lane. She has an altogether different goal: Seduction is her most potent weapon and she wields it proudly.

While food is clearly not the only ammunition in her arsenal of seduction, it's the one she prides most. While her meal choices aren't subtle in their innuendo, they are unmistakably her own. No one else on Wisteria Lane took the time to make Sausage Puttanesca and Ambrosia for Mike Delfino when he first moved to the neighborhood. To be fair, Susan Mayer would have prepared those dishes—save for two factors that Edie will happily point out. One, it wouldn't occur to her. Two, she has absolutely no talent in the kitchen and would probably have burned down her own house—instead of Edie's—if she had attempted the task.

Having been married several times, Edie knows that different foods fit different needs. Every ingredient should be chosen to remind the man that he is about to have something special—namely, Edie Britt. It's all part of the Art of Seduction. In other words, Edie picks her courses with *purpose*.

In the modern world, it's generally accepted that there are four tastes: sweet, bitter, sour, and salty. However, as the resident gourmand, Edie knows something most people don't. There is a *fifth* taste: A Japanese researcher found that the glutamate contained in seaweed sauce triggered a fifth taste the Japanese call *umami*, commonly translated as meaning "mouthwatering" or "savory." But that definition doesn't do umami justice —it's an incomparable taste sensation that encompasses all of the senses. (In fact, some tastemakers equate it with perfect sex. Perhaps Edie's fascination is understandable.)

Since this taste comes from the ocean, it is not surprising that it appears in many seafood dishes. Coincidentally, many of Edie's favorite meals revolve around dishes that contain that mouthwatering taste. To illustrate this point, let's take a look at a typical seduction à la Edie Britt:

To start off the evening with a bang, Edie will begin with her personal favorite, Oysters Poached in Champagne and Cream. (Oysters may be a cliché, but Edie can testify to the fact that they do, in fact, work as an aphrodisiac.)

Once she's pulled a man into her web, she shifts to a simple dish such as Angel Hair Pasta with Smoked Salmon. Edie has had the most success with this item, which is chock-full of umami. In fact, she rarely gets to finish it on the first round, oftentimes forced to eat it as leftovers the next day.

In the rare case that the appetizer and entrée do not "seal the deal," Edie pulls out the big guns: Molten Chocolate Cake, her specialty dessert, which will overpower any man and keep him in her proximity and at her mercy.

Like everything in her life, the meals fulfill a need and serve a purpose. Edie does not slave over a hot stove or fondue pot for *nothing*.

Edie recommends adult guidance as well as prudence before proceeding with any of the following recipes. They might be considered dangerous weapons—even weapons of mass destruction if cooked in large enough quantities—if they fall into the wrong hands. Edie takes no blame for misuse, abuse, or even *too* much success with her recipes.

Camembert Baked in Its Box

One 8-ounce whole wheel of Camembert, packed in a wooden box
1 loaf crusty baguette or Perfect Crostini (page 222)

1. Preheat the oven to 200°F.

2. Uncover the box and remove the plastic or cellophane wrapping from the cheese, leaving the rind intact. Return the cheese to the bottom of the box and set on an oven rack, uncovered, until the center is soft to the touch and the cheese is lightly warmed throughout, about 20 minutes.

3. Cover the box and bring to the table before uncovering to serve with the baguette or crostini.

SERVES 4 AS A SNACK

Perfect Crostini

Crostini are crisp and sturdy holders for toppings of all sorts, from salads made from shrimp or chicken to finely diced tomato and red onion tossed with basil and olive oil. They are also nice floated on soups, crumbled into salads, and served alongside cheeses.

1 small thin, firm loaf French bread
Olive oil
1 peeled garlic clove, cut in half (optional)

1. Set a rack in the center position and preheat the oven to 350°F.

2. Cut the bread crosswise into ½-inch slices. Brush both sides of the bread lightly with olive oil, placing them on a baking sheet as you go. If you like, rub each slice with the cut side of the garlic as well. Bake 7 minutes. Turn and bake until very crisp and lightly browned on both sides, about 10 minutes. Serve warm or cool. Crostini can be stored at room temperature in a tightly sealed container for up to 2 days.

MAKES ABOUT 24 CROSTINI

VARIATIONS

Cheesy Crostini

After turning the crostini, sprinkle the tops lightly and evenly with grated Parmesan cheese. Continue as above.

Herby Crostini

After brushing the bread slices with oil, sprinkle dried herbs such as thyme, sage, or oregano (or a mixture) lightly over the bread. Continue as above.

Warm Herbed Goat Cheese Salad
with Walnut Dressing

eathery baby arugula, sold in 5-ounce cellophane packs, is ideal here. Any other fluffy, full-flavored greens, like baby spinach or mesclun, work too.

FOR THE CHEESE

One 4-ounce log plain goat cheese

½ teaspoon dried thyme

¼ teaspoon dried sage or dried oregano

¼ teaspoon finely ground black pepper

FOR THE SALAD

2 medium heads Belgian endive (about ½ pound)

2 cups baby arugula, baby spinach, or mesclun

1 tablespoon red wine vinegar

2 teaspoons Dijon or grainy mustard

Salt and freshly ground black pepper

¼ cup walnut pieces, toasted (see page 251)

¼ cup olive oil

1. Cut the cheese crosswise into 4 rounds. Stir the thyme, sage or oregano, and pepper together on a plate until blended. Roll the cheese rounds in the mixture to coat the sides, leaving the flat top and bottom uncoated. Put the cheese rounds, flat-side down, on a small baking sheet. They can be prepared up to a day in advance and refrigerated.

2. Pull any brown or wilted leaves from the endive. Cut each head lengthwise into quarters. Cut out the core from each quarter, then separate the endive leaves. Wash the endive leaves and baby greens and dry thoroughly, preferably in a salad spinner. The greens can be stored in the vegetable crisper for up to 8 hours.

CONTINUED

3. Make the dressing: Whisk the vinegar, mustard, and a pinch each of salt and pepper together in a medium bowl until blended. In a small food processor or blender, blend the walnuts and oil until the walnuts are finely chopped and the oil is cloudy. Slowly whisk the walnut oil into the mustard mixture. Season to taste with salt and pepper.

4. To serve: Preheat the oven to 250°F. Bake the cheese until warmed and softened, about 10 minutes. Meanwhile, toss the greens and dressing together in a large mixing bowl until the endive is coated. Divide between two plates and top each serving with 2 rounds of cheese. Serve immediately.

SERVES 2 GENEROUSLY

Angel Hair Pasta with Smoked Salmon

TO APPROXIMATE
4 OUNCES OF
PASTA WITHOUT
A SCALE, STAND
THE PASTA ON
ITS END. THE
STACK WILL BE
ABOUT AS WIDE
AS A QUARTER.

Salt

2 tablespoons unsalted butter

3 tablespoons finely chopped chives or fresh dill

4 ounces angel hair pasta

2 slices smoked salmon (about 2 ounces), finely chopped (about ½ cup)

Salt and freshly ground black pepper

2 lemon wedges, seeds removed

1. Bring a large pot of salted water to a boil.

2. Meanwhile, put the butter and herb of choice in a small bowl. Set aside. Add the pasta to the boiling water and cook, stirring, until tender but still firm in the center, about 3 minutes. Spoon ¼ cup of the cooking liquid into the bowl with the butter, then drain the pasta.

3. Return the pasta to the pot but keep off the heat. Add the contents of the small bowl and toss well. Add the salmon, toss again, and season to taste with salt and pepper. Divide between two warm shallow bowls, top each with a lemon wedge, and serve immediately.

SERVES 2 AS AN APPETIZER

Oysters Poached in Champagne and Cream

If you aren't handy enough with an oyster knife to open your own oysters (or if you've just had a manicure), pulling this one off may take a little sweet-talking. (A little décolletage can't hurt either.) Start at a reputable fish store and ask if they will shuck the oysters for you, putting the shucked oysters and their juices in one container and the larger (cupped) shells in another. The flat shells can be discarded.

1 tablespoon butter

2 lightly packed cups fresh baby spinach, washed and thoroughly dried

Salt and freshly ground black pepper

¼ cup heavy cream

¼ cup dry good champagne (the rest of the bottle is for sipping with the oysters)

8 oysters, shucked, juices and cupped shells reserved

INEXPENSIVE GIZMOS FOR RECORKING A BOTTLE OF CHAMPAGNE WITHOUT LOSING ITS FIZZ ARE AVAILABLE IN COOKWARE STORES AND SOME WINE SHOPS.

1. Heat the butter in a medium skillet over medium heat until foaming. Add the spinach and cook, stirring, until wilted and bright green. Don't overcook. Season to taste lightly with salt and pepper and set aside. (The spinach can be cooked up to 1 hour in advance.)

2. Put the cream and champagne in a small saucepan. Strain the oyster liquid into the saucepan and set the oysters aside. Bring to a simmer and cook over low heat until the liquid is thick enough to lightly coat a spoon. There will be only 3 to 4 tablespoons of sauce. (The sauce can be made up to 30 minutes before serving.)

3. Set the spinach over low heat until warmed through. Set the saucepan over medium heat, add the oysters, and cook just until the edges start to curl, about 2 minutes. They will not be fully cooked. Spoon the spinach into the oyster shells, dividing it evenly. Top the spinach with a oyster. Spoon some of the oyster sauce into each shell. Serve immediately, accompanied by the remaining champagne.

LINING THE SERVING PLATES WITH A THICK LAYER OF COARSE SALT WILL KEEP THE OYSTERS STEADY WHILE SERVING.

SERVES 2

Sausage Puttanesca (with or without Pasta)

Puttanesca is an Italian adjective that describes those ladies who ply the world's oldest profession. Most often, it refers to a pasta sauce made with a lusty combination of tomatoes, garlic, anchovies, olives, and capers. As the story goes, the sauce could be easily and quickly made with ingredients kept in a pantry.

Here it is a sauce for sausages, which make a meal when paired with plain white rice or mashed potatoes. Slice the sausages and return them to the sauce and they make a fine topping for pasta.

> 4 small links (about 12 ounces) sweet or hot Italian pork or turkey sausage
> 2 tablespoons olive oil
> 2 medium garlic cloves, finely chopped
> 3 flat anchovy fillets, coarsely chopped
> 8 Italian or Greek black olives, pitted and coarsely chopped (about ¼ cup)
> 1 tablespoon tiny (nonpareil) capers, drained
> ¼ cup dry red wine
> One 14-ounce can diced tomatoes, with liquid
> Freshly ground black pepper
> 2 tablespoons chopped fresh Italian parsley

1. Poke the sausage links all over with a fork. Heat the oil in a heavy medium skillet over medium-low heat. Cook the sausages, turning as necessary, until well browned on all sides, about 8 minutes. (Some types of sausages may not be fully cooked at this point; they will finish cooking in the sauce.)

2. If necessary, pour off all but 2 tablespoons fat from the pan. Add the garlic and anchovies and cook, mashing the anchovies with a fork, until the garlic is lightly browned and the anchovies dissolve, about 2 minutes. Add the olives and capers and cook a minute or two.

3. Increase the heat to high, pour in the wine, and boil until almost completely evaporated. Stir in the tomatoes and bring to a boil. Tuck the sausages into the sauce, adjust the heat so the sauce is simmering, and cover. Cook, turning the sausages once or twice, 10 minutes. Check the seasoning. Because of the olives, anchovies, and capers, you most likely won't have to add salt. But a little freshly ground black pepper would be nice. Sprinkle the parsley over the sausages and serve them hot, spooning some of the sauce over each serving.

VARIATION

Sausage Puttanesca with Pasta

Remove the pan from the heat. Cut the sausages into ½-inch lengths and return them to the sauce. Makes enough to sauce 8 ounces (half a package) of a chunky pasta shape such as rigatoni, radiatore, or large shells, which makes 2 very generous portions or 4 regular portions.

SERVES 2 AS IS OR 2 TO 4 AS A SAUCE FOR PASTA

Herb and Lemon Roasted Chicken

One 4 ½-pound free-range, organic, or kosher chicken
Salt and freshly ground black pepper
1 lemon, cut into quarters
2 to 3 rosemary, thyme, and/or sage sprigs (any or all)
6 unpeeled garlic cloves

1. Remove the giblets and neck from the cavity of the chicken. Pull out the pockets of fat from the cavity. Rinse the chicken inside and out under cold water; drain the chicken thoroughly, then pat it dry inside and out with paper towels. Put the chicken in a roasting pan large enough to hold it comfortably. Season the chicken inside and out generously with salt and pepper. Set the chicken, breast-side up, in the pan and tuck the lemon pieces, herbs, and garlic into the cavity. Let the chicken stand at room temperature 30 minutes.

2. Meanwhile, preheat the oven to 450°F. Roast the chicken until very well browned and no trace of pink remains near the joint where the thigh meets the backbone, about 1 hour (see box below). Let stand 10 minutes before serving.

3. The simplest way to serve a roasted chicken is to pull the legs away from the body to expose the joint where the thigh meets the backbone. Cut off the legs with a knife or kitchen shears and arrange on a platter. Do the same with the wings. Cut along the backbone to separate it from the breast and then either carve thin slices from the breast or use the kitchen shears to cut the whole breast into halves.

SERVES 4

Time and Temperature

The best way to be sure a chicken—or any other poultry or meat—is properly cooked is to test the temperature. Instant-reading dial or digital thermometers are very reasonably priced (reliable ones go for about ten bucks) and will last quite a while. In the case of chicken or turkey, the bird is fully cooked, not to mention safe to eat, when the temperature of the thickest part of the thigh near the bone reaches 165°F.

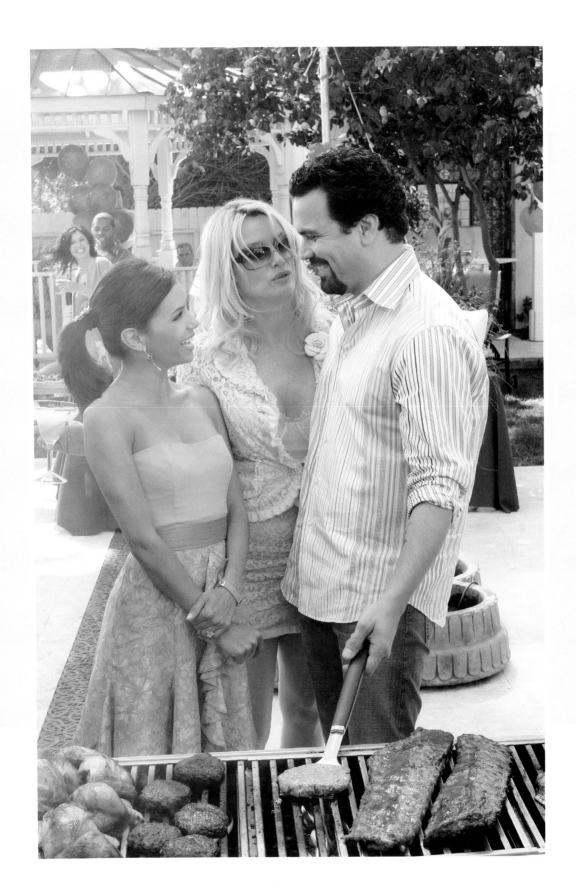

Ambrosia

In the south, ambrosia is the subject of great passion. Purists insist that *real* ambrosia contains only two ingredients: oranges and shredded coconut. Others insist that seedless grapes, cut in half; thinly sliced bananas; and other fruit can be added to the mix. Here is the classic version Edie prefers (that has been "successful" in her dealings).

3 Valencia oranges
Superfine sugar (optional)
½ cup coarsely shredded coconut (see Note)

1. Cut both ends off the oranges. Stand them flat on a cutting board and, using a paring knife, cut off the peel and white pith but remove as little of the orange flesh as possible. Working over a bowl, use the paring knife to cut the segments free of the membrane and let the segments drop into the bowl. Squeeze all the juice out of the membranes and over the segments once you've freed all the segments.

2. Make a layer of orange segments in a small glass serving bowl or in each of two individual glass dishes. Sprinkle lightly with sugar if you like. Top with coconut and repeat, using all the orange segments and coconut. Drizzle the juice over the top. Cover and refrigerate at least 4 hours but no longer than 1 day. Serve chilled.

SERVES 2

Note: Unsweetened coconut, shaved into large thin ripples, is available in some specialty and health food stores. (Also see Sources, page 266.) It looks beautiful in ambrosia and lends a very nice texture as well.

the hottie from the physical therapist's office

the blond guy at the butcher's shop ♡

the new UPS delivery man

the old UPS delivery man

New York steaks

whipped cream

Power bars

Multivitamins

sprouted grain bread

Chocolate sauce

fresh vegetables

Raspberry pie

Ready-Pak salad

low-fat salad dressing

Jumbo shrimp

turkey deli meat

Fresca

Fuji water

eggs

Cabernet Sauvignon

Morning Star veggie
corn dogs

Corona Light

Champagne

disposable champagne
flutes

800-count Egyptian
cotton sheets

Vitamin B12

Molten Chocolate Cake

Here is one of those huge restaurant trends that migrated into the home kitchens of Wisteria Lane and the rest of the country. Orchestrating a crispy exterior with a soft, runny interior may seem like quite a feat, but it is really very simple. Unmolding the cakes onto plates is a little tricky, though, and if you plan to do this for company, a trial run well before dinner is in order.

4 tablespoons unsalted butter, plus more for the baking dishes
¼ cup sugar, plus more for the baking dishes
2 ounces bittersweet chocolate, cut or broken into ½-inch pieces
2 large eggs
2 tablespoons all-purpose flour

1. Set a rack in the center position and preheat the oven to 400°F. Butter the insides of two 8-ounce ceramic or glass baking dishes. Sprinkle with the sugar to coat the insides and set them on a baking sheet.

2. Put the butter and chocolate in the top of a double boiler or a heatproof bowl. Set over simmering water and heat, stirring occasionally, until the butter and chocolate are melted and smooth. Remove and set aside.

3. Beat the eggs and ¼ cup sugar together in a bowl with a handheld mixer at high speed until pale yellow, fluffy, and about tripled in volume. Scrape the chocolate mixture into the egg mixture and sift the flour over the top. Fold the ingredients together with a rubber spatula until thoroughly blended.

4. Divide the batter between the prepared baking dishes. Bake just until risen, a crack or two appears on the top of each, and just the center is runny, about 12 minutes. Remove and let stand 2 minutes.

5. To serve: The cakes should be served hot to warm. The longer the cakes sit, the more the center will firm up. Even if you serve them when the centers are completely firm, the cakes will still be delicious. They can be served right in the baking dish or, for the adventurous, removed from the baking dish and served on plates. To remove from the dish, line one hand with a clean towel. Using a

CONTINUED

potholder or dishcloth, grasp the baking dish with the other hand and invert the cake onto the clean cloth. Lift the dish, then set the cake, right-side up, on the plate. Because of the soft center, the cake may sag a little. That is fine; the runny center that oozes out onto the plate when the cakes are cut more than makes up for that.

SERVES 2 (THE RECIPE CAN BE EASILY DOUBLED OR TRIPLED.)

Note: The batter can be prepared, poured into the dishes, and refrigerated for up to 1 day. Bake refrigerated cakes at 375°F for 15 minutes and proceed as above.

Edie on Scents

In recent years, studies have been made on various scents and their effects on people. Scientists have studied the increase in penile blood flow when men were exposed to various scents. In the first round, cinnamon was the big winner, but in the end, lavender and pumpkin pie increased the test subject's penile blood flow by 40 percent. Needless to say, soon after Edie came across the study (and surprise, surprise, she does follow these things), pumpkin pie was added to her favorite desserts and lavender became the scent of choice in her bedroom.

Make-Your-Own Sundae (Ice Cream Optional)

When company (of the male variety) is over, Edie has been known to forget the ice cream and merely enjoy the toppings. We recommend you try the classic version printed below.

FOR THE WET WALNUTS (MAKES 1 1/2 CUPS)

½ cup sugar

½ cup maple syrup

1 ½ cups coarsely chopped walnut halves or pieces

FOR THE EASIEST CHOCOLATE SAUCE (MAKES 3/4 CUP)

4 ounces bittersweet chocolate

½ cup heavy cream

Ice cream(s) of choice

ADDITIONAL TOPPINGS

Whipped cream

Maraschino cherries

Jimmies or candy sprinkles

1. Make the wet walnuts: Bring the sugar and ¾ cup water to a boil, stirring, over medium heat. Add the maple syrup, return to a boil, and cook 3 minutes. Remove from the heat and stir in the walnuts. The walnuts can be kept in a covered container at room temperature.

2. Make the chocolate sauce: Break the chocolate into smallish pieces, dropping them into a small, heavy saucepan. Pour in the cream. Heat over very low heat until the chocolate is melted. Whisk until smooth and glossy. Serve warm. (The chocolate sauce can be prepared up to several hours in advance. Cover the saucepan and keep at room temperature, then rewarm over low heat before serving. Scrape into a storage container and refrigerate for longer keeping.)

3. Bring the ice cream(s) to room temperature about 10 minutes before scooping. Meanwhile, rewarm the toppings if necessary. Scoop the ice cream into bowls or sundae dishes and top with one or both of the sauces. Dress as you like with any or all of the additional toppings.

The Neighbors

Our focus

has been on our favorite
Desperate Housewives of
Wisteria Lane, but believe it
or not, there are other people
living on the street as well.
They come in and out of our
favorite housewives' lives,
some for better, some for
worse. Here are a few of
their favorite recipes.

Mrs. Huber

The late Martha Huber was known for many things around the neighborhood: being a busybody, borrowing items she never planned on returning, and blackmailing the late Mary Alice Young among the most well known (although only the tip of the iceberg). But one thing she was never known for was her cooking. Even the late Mr. Huber would have been surprised to learn that she fancied herself a great chef. Of course, he felt this way because the only thing she ever gave him was heartburn and it generally wasn't her cooking that caused it. . . .

However, Martha had her strengths in the kitchen. In fact, the very thing that eventually caused her demise was used in her favorite dish, the Martha Huber Strawberry Smoothie Surprise.

Strawberry Smoothie

1 cup frozen strawberries (loose, not in syrup)
½ cup vanilla or plain yogurt
½ cup orange juice
1 package artificial sweetener (optional)

Combine the strawberries, yogurt, and orange juice in a blender jar. Blend until the strawberries are coarsely chopped. Increase the speed to high and blend, adding water 1 tablespoon at a time, until the smoothie is smooth but very thick. You will need from 3 to 6 tablespoons water. Add the sweetener if you like, Mrs. Huber would say with a smile. Nothing can be *too* sweet. Pour into a tall chilled glass and drink right away.

MAKES 1 SMOOTHIE

Yellow Cake

BLEACHED FLOUR CONTAINS A LITTLE LESS PRO- TEIN THAN UNBLEACHED AND MAKES A SLIGHTLY MORE TENDER CAKE.

2 sticks (16 tablespoons) unsalted butter, plus more for the cake pans,
    at room temperature

2 ¼ cups bleached all-purpose flour, plus more for the cake pans

2 teaspoons baking powder

½ teaspoon salt

1 ½ cups sugar

4 large eggs, at room temperature

2 teaspoons pure vanilla extract

⅔ cup milk

1. Set a rack in the center position and preheat the oven to 350°F. Butter two 9-inch cake pans well. Add a heaping tablespoon of flour to one and rotate and tap the pan to coat it lightly with flour. Tap the excess into the second pan and flour that one.

2. Sift the flour, baking powder, and salt into a bowl. Set aside. Beat the butter and sugar in the bowl of an electric mixer (or in a bowl with a handheld mixer) at high speed until very light and fluffy, about 5 minutes. Add the eggs one at a time, beating for a minute after each. Beat in the vanilla.

3. Fold in half of the dry ingredients. Add in the milk and then the remaining dry ingredients, and fold just until a streak or two of dry ingredients remain. Don't overmix. Scrape the batter into the prepared pans, dividing it evenly.

4. Bake until the top is lightly browned and a wooden pick inserted into the center of each cake comes out clean, about 30 minutes. Cool on a rack for 15 minutes.

5. Invert the layers onto the rack, lift off the pan, and cool completely before eating or frosting.

MAKES TWO 9-INCH LAYERS OR 16 TO 24 CUPCAKES (SEE NOTE)

TO MAKE CUPCAKES:

If using standard paper cupcake baking cups, use them to line muffin tins (see page 60). The batter will make about 20 plump cupcakes or 24 flat-topped cupcakes. New arrivals on the scene are silvery, sturdy baking cups, which need no muffin tins; they stand freely on a baking sheet. They also hold more batter than traditional paper cups. This batter will make about 16 cupcakes using freestanding cups. Whichever type you use, fill the cups about three-quarters full with batter. Cupcakes baked in muffin tins with paper cups will take about 20 minutes; those baked in freestanding silver cups, about 25 minutes.

Chocolate Frosting

Plain and simple, much like Martha Huber herself (but without the bitterness), this recipe requires no cooking (just melting) and no special equipment. Martha would have recommended using the frosting as soon as it is made and then refrigerating the frosted cake or cupcakes.

8 ounces semisweet chocolate

1 ½ sticks (12 tablespoons) unsalted butter, at room temperature, cut into 8 pieces

⅔ cup confectioners' sugar

1 ½ teaspoons pure vanilla extract

1. If using individually wrapped boxed chocolate, snap each square in half. If using block chocolate, cut it into rough chunks. Drop the chocolate in the top of a double boiler or large heatproof bowl. Set over a pot of barely simmering water and heat, stirring occasionally, until the chocolate is about three-quarters melted. Remove and stir until the chocolate is completely melted.

2. Add the butter to the chocolate and beat at high speed with a handheld mixer until the butter is fully incorporated. Add the confectioners' sugar and vanilla and beat at low speed until blended. Increase the speed to high and beat until the frosting lightens and becomes a little fluffier. Refrigerate the cake or cupcakes after frosting. Remove them to room temperature 30 to 45 minutes before serving.

MAKES 2 CUPS, ENOUGH TO FROST TWO 9-INCH LAYERS
OR 24 CUPCAKES

Date Nut Bread

Martha Huber was the last person on Wisteria Lane to keep the tradition of Date Nut Bread—seemingly on the endangered species list for breads—alive. With her untimely and unseemly passing, this is your chance to keep the recipe going.

Vegetable oil cooking spray
2 cups chopped pitted dates (about 10 ounces)
1 teaspoon baking soda
⅓ cup molasses
2 cups all-purpose flour
¾ cup chopped walnuts
1 teaspoon baking powder
1 large egg
½ cup granulated sugar
¼ cup brown sugar

1. Place a rack in the center position and heat the oven to 350°F. Grease a 9 x 5 x 4-inch loaf pan liberally with cooking spray.

2. Toss the dates and baking soda together in a large bowl. Heat the molasses and ⅔ cup water just to boiling. Pour over the dates; the liquid will foam up dramatically. Let stand until cool.

3. Stir the flour, walnuts, and baking powder together in a small bowl. Beat the egg until frothy and stir into the date liquid, then stir in the sugars. Add the flour mixture and stir just until blended. Don't overmix.

4. Spoon the batter into the prepared pan. Tap lightly to settle the batter. Bake until risen and a long wooden pick or skewer inserted into the center of the bread is removed clean, about 1 hour. Remove and cool completely.

5. Remove from the pan and wrap tightly in plastic wrap. Store at room temperature for up to 3 days or wrap in foil and freeze for up to 1 month.

MAKES 1 LOAF, ABOUT 12 SLICES

Mike

Resident hunk, neighborhood plumber, and all-around good guy (albeit one who carries a gun), Mike Delfino does not give much thought to spending time in the kitchen. Over the last few years, he's been quite busy: Between the search for his late ex-wife, his quest to connect with his son, and his on-again/off-again roller coaster of a romance with Susan Mayer, he has his plate full. That said, Mike is from Tennessee and, as such, favors traditional barbecue and a good cut of meat above all else. The one dish he is most proud of is his rib eye steak with onion gravy. And since Mike is always willing to share, here is the recipe, available for the first time to the world outside Wisteria Lane.

Mike's Rib Eye Steak with Onion Gravy

One well-trimmed 14-ounce rib eye steak, about 1 ¼ inches thick
Salt and freshly ground black pepper
Vegetable oil
1 small yellow onion, thinly sliced (about ¾ cup)
½ cup beer (any type)

1. Dry the steak well with paper towels. Rub the steak generously with salt and pepper on both sides and let stand at room temperature 30 minutes.

2. Pour enough oil into a large, heavy pan to generously coat the bottom. Heat over medium-high heat just until the oil begins to smoke. Quickly and carefully lay the steak in the pan. Cover the pan to reduce splattering and cook until the underside is very well browned, about 5 minutes. Reduce the heat to medium, flip the steak, and cook until done to your liking, about 4 minutes for a medium-rare steak. Transfer to a plate.

3. Discard the fat from the pan. Return the pan to the heat, add the onion, and season lightly with salt and pepper. Cook, stirring, until the onion is wilted and golden brown, about 3 minutes. Pour in the beer and cook until almost completely evaporated. Remove from the heat and pour in any juices from the plate.

4. Cut the steak on a 45-degree angle into ½-inch slices. Divide the steak between two warm plates and flank each serving with half the onions and juice. Serve immediately.

SERVES 2 (DATE-SIZE PORTIONS) OR 1 (STAG PORTION)

Felicia

Felicia Tillman is known around the neighborhood primarily as Martha Huber's sister—not something of which she is particularly proud. Ask her about her nursing career or the men she almost married and Felicia will be slightly more forthcoming, but she is far from a blabbermouth. However, if you query her about her culinary expertise—which, for some reason, no one ever seems to do—she will regale you with tales of her Banana Walnut Bread winning the prize at the local cook-off. If you find her at a particularly garrulous moment (meaning you have not mentioned her sister), she will tell you the secrets of her Double Whammy Chocolate Pudding and Vanilla Pudding recipes. Here, for the first time, are Felicia Tillman's recipes in all their glory.

Banana Walnut Bread

Vegetable oil cooking spray

2 cups all-purpose flour, plus more for the pan

3 large, very ripe bananas

2 teaspoons fresh lemon juice

1 ½ teaspoons baking powder

½ teaspoon salt

1 cup coarsely chopped walnuts, toasted

8 tablespoons (1 stick) unsalted butter, at room temperature

¾ cup sugar

2 large eggs

¼ cup milk

1 teaspoon pure vanilla extract or 1 tablespoon rum

TO TOAST WALNUTS, SPREAD THEM OUT ON A BAKING SHEET AND TOAST, STIRRING ONCE, IN A 350°F OVEN UNTIL EVENLY LIGHT GOLDEN BROWN, ABOUT 12 MINUTES.

1. Spray an 8 x 4 x 4-inch loaf pan with cooking spray. Put about a tablespoon of flour in the pan and tap and rotate the pan to coat the inside of the pan with flour. Set aside. Set a rack in the center position of the oven and preheat the oven to 350°F.

2. Peel the bananas, cut them into thirds, and put in a food processor. Add the lemon juice and process until smooth. Set aside 1 cup banana purée. If there is ¼ cup or more extra purée, you may use it to make a glaze for the finished bread (see page 252).

3. Stir the flour, baking powder, and salt together in a mixing bowl. Add the walnuts and stir to coat with flour.

4. Beat the butter and sugar together until light and fluffy. Add the eggs one at a time, beating thoroughly after each. Beat in the reserved banana purée, milk, and vanilla until smooth. Fold in the flour mixture just until no streaks of flour remain. Scrape the batter into the prepared pan and bake until a wooden pick inserted into the center of the cake comes out clean, about 1 hour.

CONTINUED

5. Cool on a rack in the pan for 15 minutes. Invert the cake onto the rack, remove the pan, and set the bread upright on the rack. Cool completely.

6. To make the glaze: Beat enough confectioners' sugar into the remaining banana purée to make a glaze thick enough to heavily coat a spoon. You will need about ⅓ cup sugar for every ¼ cup purée. When the bread is completely cool, spread the glaze generously over the top, allowing it to drip down the sides. With or without glaze, serve the cake in thick slices. Wrapped or covered, the cake will keep at room temperature for up to 3 days.

MAKES ONE 9-INCH LOAF, ABOUT 10 SLICES

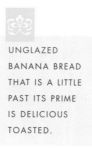

UNGLAZED
BANANA BREAD
THAT IS A LITTLE
PAST ITS PRIME
IS DELICIOUS
TOASTED.

Almond Macaroons

S lightly chewy, simple to put together, and universally loved, these are a welcome addition to any cookie repertoire. Look for 7-ounce tubes, not 8-ounce cans, of almond paste. Tubes are easy to squeeze and they ensure that the paste is soft and fresh. Don't confuse almond paste with marzipan. They are often sold side by side but are quite different.

¾ cup superfine sugar
¼ cup slivered almonds
2 tablespoons cornstarch
2 large egg whites
One 7-ounce tube almond paste, cut into small pieces
Maraschino cherries, cut into thin slivers, or finely chopped
   peeled almonds (optional)

1. Put the sugar, almonds, and cornstarch in a food processor. Process the almonds to a fine powder. Add the egg whites and process until smooth. Add the almond paste and purée until completely smooth. Store the batter in a covered container, refrigerated, for at least 4 hours or up to 3 days.

2. Preheat the oven to 300°F. Use a nonstick baking sheet or a baking sheet lined with parchment paper. Transfer the batter to a pastry tube fitted with a wide star tip. Pipe 1 ½-inch stars onto the baking sheet, leaving 1 inch between them. (Alternately, drop the batter by rounded tablespoons onto the sheet.) Top each with a sliver of maraschino cherry or a light sprinkling of chopped almonds, if using.

3. Bake until the cookies are lightly browned in places and a macaroon feels light when picked up, 30 to 35 minutes. Remove immediately to a wire rack to cool. Cool completely before serving. Macaroons can be stored in an airtight container at room temperature for 5 days.

MAKES ABOUT 24 MACAROONS

Double Whammy Chocolate Pudding

2 cups milk

2 tablespoons cornstarch

½ cup sugar

⅓ cup cocoa

2 large eggs

2 teaspoons pure vanilla extract

4 ounces semisweet or bittersweet chocolate, coarsely chopped

1. Stir ¼ cup of the milk and the cornstarch together in a small bowl until the cornstarch is dissolved. Set aside

2. Whisk the remaining milk, sugar, and cocoa together in a heavy 2-quart saucepan. Place over medium-low heat and continue whisking until the milk is steaming and the sugar and cocoa are dissolved. Stir the cornstarch mixture again and pour it into the saucepan. Continue cooking and stirring, paying special attention to the corners, until the mixture comes to a simmer. Adjust the heat to low and cook, stirring, 1 minute.

3. Remove the pan from the heat. Beat the eggs and vanilla together in a small mixing bowl until blended. Dribble a ladleful of the hot milk mixture into the eggs while beating constantly. Scrape the egg mixture into the pan, return to the heat, and cook, stirring well, 1 minute. Remove from the heat and stir in the chocolate until melted and evenly distributed.

4. Pour the pudding into individual bowls or cups or one large serving bowl. Cover with plastic wrap. To prevent a skin from forming on the surface of the pudding, press the plastic to the surface of the pudding. Chill thoroughly.

MAKES ABOUT 3 CUPS, ENOUGH FOR 4 SERVINGS
OR 1 BATCH OF WISTERIA LANE ICEBOX NAPOLEONS (PAGE 256)

Vanilla Pudding

2 cups milk
1 cup light cream
½ cup sugar
¼ cup cornstarch
2 large eggs
2 egg yolks
1 tablespoon pure vanilla extract

1. Heat the milk and cream in a medium saucepan over medium-low heat until steaming. Meanwhile, stir the sugar and cornstarch together in a medium mixing bowl until blended. Add the eggs and egg yolks and beat until blended.

2. Slowly pour about half the milk mixture into the egg mixture, whisking constantly until smooth. Pour the egg mixture into the saucepan and cook, stirring constantly with a whisk—paying attention to the corners where the pudding can stick and scorch—until a few bubbles rise to the surface here and there. Remove from the heat and whisk for a minute or two. Pour through a sieve into a clean bowl and whisk in the vanilla. Press a sheet of plastic wrap onto the surface and cool to room temperature.

3. Refrigerate as is or spoon into serving bowls first. Chill thoroughly. The pudding will last up to 5 days if kept refrigerated.

MAKES ABOUT 3 ½ CUPS, ENOUGH FOR 4 SERVINGS
OR 1 BATCH OF WISTERIA LANE ICEBOX NAPOLEONS (PAGE 256)

Wisteria Lane Icebox Napoleons

Once upon a time, icebox cakes, made by layering chocolate wafers and whipped cream in a cake pan, ruled. After a good night's rest, the cookies became moistened by the cream and the whole firmed up enough to cut into neat little slices. Here is a similar idea, made with chocolate or vanilla pudding layered with graham crackers. If you're making the napoleons with vanilla pudding, think about using cinnamon-flavored graham crackers in place of the plain.

IN A PINCH, PACKAGED PUDDING CAN BE SUBSTITUTED FOR HOMEMADE.

**Double Whammy Chocolate Pudding (page 254)
  or Vanilla Pudding (page 255)
About ½ a 14-ounce box plain or cinnamon-flavored graham crackers
Confectioners' sugar or cocoa (optional)**

1. Make the pudding and cool to room temperature with a piece of plastic wrap pressed directly to the surface to prevent a skin from forming.

2. Line the bottom of an 8 x 8-inch cake pan or baking dish with graham crackers. Spread half the pudding over the crackers. Then top with another layer of crackers and the remaining pudding. Finish with a layer of crackers. Cover the pan tightly and refrigerate at least 6 hours or up to overnight.

3. Dust the top of the napoleons with confectioners' sugar or cocoa if you like. Cut into 9 squares and serve cold.

SERVES 9

Mrs. McCluskey

Mrs. McCluskey is not someone you want to cross. Many a neighbor on Wisteria Lane has felt her wrath. Few to none have seen her soft side, save for Lynette on one particularly bad day last year and, one assumes, Mrs. McCluskey's late husband. He was possibly the only one who knew about her one weakness—peanut brittle—and how it caused her to stop complaining . . . for a few minutes at least.

Perhaps it is the fact that her mouth is kept busy with all the requisite chewing that peanut brittle demands, but Mrs. McCluskey seems to be a different person when she is preparing and eating her favorite snack. If only the neighbors could find a way to make this a full-time occupation . . .

Mrs. McCluskey's Peanut Brittle

Vegetable oil
2 cups sugar
½ cup light corn syrup
2 tablespoons unsalted butter
1 ½ teaspoons baking powder
1 ½ cups salted or unsalted dry-roasted peanuts

1. Generously oil a baking sheet and a flat metal spatula. Set aside. Have ready a bowl of cold water and a pastry brush. Stir the sugar, corn syrup, and ¼ cup water together in a heavy 3-quart saucepan. Bring to a boil over medium heat, stirring just until the sugar is dissolved. Boil without stirring, but washing down any sugar crystals that form on the sides of the pan using the brush dipped in water, until the temperature of the syrup reaches 295°F. The syrup will be very pale brown.

2. Drop in the butter pieces and wiggle the pan very gently to swirl the butter into the syrup. The syrup will foam up and cool; continue cooking until the syrup reaches 300°F.

3. Remove from the heat and stir in the baking powder. Be careful; the syrup will foam up. Stir in the nuts, then immediately pour the contents of the pan onto the prepared baking sheet, spreading it into a thin even layer with the oiled spatula. Cool completely.

4. Slip the oiled spatula between the brittle and baking sheet. Use a rolling pin or meat tenderizer to break the brittle into small pieces. Store in an airtight container for up to 2 weeks.

MAKES ABOUT THIRTY 2-INCH PIECES

Note: This is an old-fashioned peanut brittle—creamy, pale tan with a touch of richness from the butter. A candy thermometer—which also comes in handy for checking the temperature of oil for frying—is necessary. Salted peanuts make a nice contrast to the sweetness.

From Snack Food to Haute Cuisine:

A View from the Set of *Desperate Housewives*

Making the food on *Desperate Housewives* look as mouthwatering and appetizing as it appears on television every week is no easy feat. It takes a team of people, a mountain of money, and anywhere from twelve to twenty exact duplicates of each dish seen on film for the simplest scene involving any form of food.

Because each meal seen onscreen has to be practical—edible and preferably something the actor is not just willing but eager to ingest—it has a limited life span on the set. Unlike in commercials, where food stylists often prepare things that will look good on the screen but are not fit for human consumption, food on a TV series must be not just edible, but tasty—and look good on screen, even in high definition.

April Falzone Garen, the food stylist, spends much of her week preparing various foods for everything from Bree's dinner parties to restaurant scenes and everything else involving anything edible. Having worked on such features as *Mr. & Mrs. Smith* and *Catch Me If You Can*, as well as on numerous TV shows, Mrs. Garen has her work cut out for her on *Desperate Housewives*, particularly if a scene calls for Bree Van De Kamp to prepare one of her lavish dinner parties. Point of fact, every episode contains some element of food—from cookies in the Scavo kitchen to margaritas in the Solis bedroom. All require time, preparation, and care in order to pull off.

TOOLS OF THE TRADE

Let's look inside the food stylist's basic kit:

Knives

Carving utensils

Cutting board

Plastic wrap

Paper towels

Miniature gardening tools

Toothpicks

Parchment paper

Baking string

Little paintbrushes (for frosting cake)

A propane torch (to make things look crispy or just to add color)

A zester (to make lemon curls to decorate a plate)

Paprika (to add color and taste)

The process starts when the property master, Melody Miller-Melton, gets the script from the writers. She scours the script for any scene that has food written into it, or takes place in a room where food is expected to be or would fill out a set or scene.

Once the script is broken down into elements that require the services of the food stylist, April can get to work. This usually involves preparing and cooking everything from cookies to bouillabaisse to potato balls.

Part of the stylist's job sometimes entails teaching the actors how to cook and bake. If a scene requires a character to cook a gourmet meal, April will half-cook the item and then show the actor how to finish it so it looks perfect on camera.

On the other hand, Susan Mayer is not a good cook, so April's task is quite different. Her team's job is to utilize creative techniques to make her food look as bad as possible. To simulate an overcooked steak, they might burn it with a propane torch. To showcase how poorly she cooked her steamed broccoli and carrots, they would overcook the vegetables to make them limp and pale. One other quick and easy method they use: Add lemon juice on top of green vegetables to make them look terrible as fast as possible.

Although the department's job is mainly to make the food look *good* (see the tips on the opposite page), let's focus on an example of how they made food look bad exceedingly well. In "Running to Stand Still," an episode from Season One, they had to create an unappetizing Mexican specialty for a major plot device: For the infamous "burrito scene" in the hotel room where Bree tries to seduce her husband, Rex, only to find herself unable to get in the mood because of the food item, the entire department had to work together to create a disgusting burrito that would ooze yellow and white cheese on cue. The team had to build an apparatus with a heated tube they could insert inside the flour tortilla so that the cheese would pour out on command. This scene had to be reshot *three* times, since the director and executive producers were unhappy with the speed and volume of the cheese that was oozing out of the (nonedible) burrito.

Food Stylist Tips:
How to Make Your Food
Look Good Onscreen

The following items are not edible.

- To bring out the shine in vegetables, food stylists will coat them in Vaseline.
- Food will sometimes be undercooked in order to better maintain its shape.
- If the actors are not eating the food in the scene, the stylist might glaze it to give the food a freshly baked and just-out-of-the-oven look. Pam spray is their favorite.
- Float fried eggs in oil. They will look fresh for days.
- Fake ice cream: Use mashed potatoes or cornstarch shaped like ice cream.

As a rule, food stylists like to stay away from meat and fish, which go bad relatively quickly. In addition, many actors are vegetarians, so April has to dress their soy-based food to resemble other dishes or make sure that something they like is on the plate for the scene. Carrots and green beans are a good example.

It takes more than three industrial-size refrigerators, portable sinks, a multitude of hot plates, and the round-the-clock work of the entire prop department to pull off the enticing and appetizing look of the varieties of food that appear on *Desperate Housewives*. The fact that April is the mother of triplet teenagers probably helps her with the multitasking inherent in this line of work. From the ever-shifting work schedules to the voluminous amount of food that needs to be prepared on a daily basis (and often wasted, since it would violate health codes to feed the food props to the crew), hers is a surprisingly difficult and demanding vocation. The only reward she seeks is for viewers around the world to come away from an episode hungry. Then April and the entire prop department will know that they have succeeded.

Fun Facts

- To hold down sandwiches on a tray that a character is carrying, a small amount of cream cheese will be stuck to the bottom of the sandwich.

- Toothpicks are put in sandwiches to keep them from moving around.

- Whipped cream will be hand whipped and mixed with Splenda to lower the calories.

- Due to continuity—the art of making sure every take looks exactly like the one before it—thirty to forty edible versions of the food that appears in the scene must be made.

- In the episode where Susan purposefully overcooked Dr. Ron's steak, they had sixteen to twenty steaks at the ready. But they were all too easy to cut, so they had to insert toothpicks horizontally to make it as difficult as possible for guest star Jay Harrington to cut.

- In another episode, Lynette had to eat raw bacon. In cases where the food is also a plot element, the prop department has to "audition" the food. Melody had to order a special cured and smoked bacon from Germany. Then they took the cut to the butcher to cut it to resemble raw bacon.

- April will sample all the food to make sure it tastes as delicious as possible.

- In scenes with salads, she never puts dressing on top. Salad dressing makes lettuce limp.

SOURCES

Chili powder
Adobo sauce and/or canned chipotles in adobo sauce
Masa for tamales
Canned diced chilies
Dried corn husks
Mexican chocolate
Smoked and hot paprika

www.mexgrocer.com

Dried sliced porcini mushrooms
Italian arborio rice
"Instant" polenta

www.igourmet.com

Buckwheat flour
Shaved unsweetened coconut
Coconut milk or "light" coconut milk
Smoked and hot paprika

www.kalustyans.com

Panko

www.asianfoodgrocer.com

INDEX

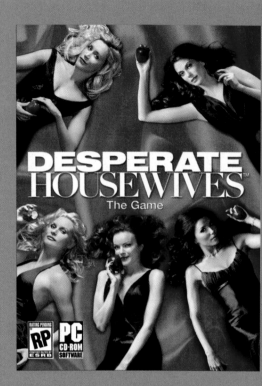

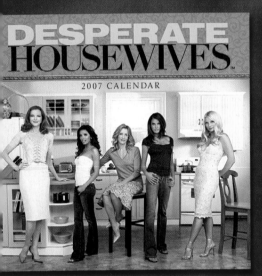
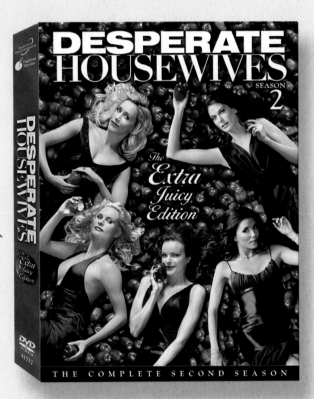